A Time to Live

A Time to Live

Seven Tasks
of
Creative Aging

Robert Raines

A DUTTON BOOK

DUTTON
Published by the Penguin Group
Penguin Books USA Inc., 375 Hudson Street,
New York, New York 10014, U.S.A.
Penguin Books Ltd, 27 Wrights Lane, London W8 5TZ, England
Penguin Books Australia Ltd, Ringwood, Victoria, Australia
Penguin Books Canada Ltd, 10 Alcorn Avenue, Toronto, Ontario, Canada M4V 3B2
Penguin Books (N.Z.) Ltd, 182–190 Wairau Road, Auckland 10, New Zealand

Penguin Books Ltd, Registered Offices:
Harmondsworth, Middlesex, England

First published by Dutton, an imprint of Dutton Signet,
a division of Penguin Books USA Inc.
Distributed in Canada by McClelland & Stewart Inc.

First Printing, May, 1997
1   3   5   7   9   10   8   6   4   2

"Ramage for Awakening Sorrow" by Robert Bly, from Angels in Pompeii, edited by Stephen
Brigidi. Copyright © 1992 by Robert Bly and Stephen Brigidi. Reprinted by permission of Ballantine
Books, a Division of Random House Inc.
Lines from "Natural Resources," from The Dream of a Common Language: Poems 1974–1977
by Adrienne Rich. Copyright © 1978 by W. W. Norton & Company, Inc. Reprinted by permission
of the author and W. W. Norton & Company, Inc.
"Poet and Person" (3 lines) by Denise Levertov, from Candles in Babylon. Copyright © 1982 by
Denise Levertov. Reprinted by permission of New Directions Publishing Corp.
"Do Not Go Gentle into That Good Night" (3 lines) by Dylan Thomas, from The Poems of
Dylan Thomas. Copyright © 1952 by Dylan Thomas. Reprinted by permission of
New Directions Publishing Corp.
"Whatever is foreseen in joy," from Sabbaths by Wendell Berry. Copyright © 1987 by Wendell
Berry. Reprinted by permission of North Point Press, a division of Farrar, Straus & Giroux, Inc.
Excerpt from "Manifesto: The Mad Farmer Liberation Front" in The Country of Marriage,
copyright © 1973 by Wendell Berry, reprinted by permission of Harcourt Brace & Company.
"Lovers (II): Reminder" by Denise Levertov, from Oblique Prayers. Copyright © 1984 by Denise
Levertov. Reprinted by permission of New Directions Publishing Corp.
"A Third Body," from Loving a Woman in Two Worlds by Robert Bly. Copyright © 1985 by
Robert Bly. Used by permission of Doubleday, a division of Bantam Doubleday Dell
Publishing Group, Inc.
Excerpt from Beloved by Toni Morrison, reprinted by permission of International Creative
Management, Inc. Copyright © 1987.
"The Cardinals" by Loren Eiseley reprinted with the permission of Scribner, a Division of Simon &
Schuster, from Notes of an Alchemist by Loren Eiseley. Copyright © 1972 by Loren Eiseley.

   REGISTERED TRADEMARK—MARCA REGISTRADA

LIBRARY OF CONGRESS CATALOGING-IN-PUBLICATION DATA:
Raines, Robert Arnold.
    A time to live : seven tasks of creative aging / Robert Raines.
        p.   cm.
    Includes bibliographical references.
    ISBN 0-525-94283-1 (alk. paper)
    1. Self-actualization (Psychology) in old age. 2. Aging—Psychological aspects. 3. Maturation
(Psychology) I. Title.
BF724.85.S45R35   1997
155.67—dc21   96-39771
                                                                                                    CIP

Printed in the United States of America
Set in Bembo
Designed by Jesse Cohen

For Cindy
sweet companion
of these years

CONTENTS

ACKNOWLEDGMENTS

I wish to thank my agent, James Levine, for believing in this book and guiding me to my publisher, and my editor, Arnold Dolin, for his encouragement and careful work on the book. I want to thank readers of the manuscript in its early forms: Cynthia Hirni, Kathleen Fischer, David Dodson Gray, Joan Hemenway, and Walter Wink. Their judgments and suggestions substantially improved the book. I am grateful to the many participants in Elder Passage workshops over the years, and to members of my family, colleagues, and friends, from whom I learned much about myself and aging, and by whose generosity the reader is allowed glimpses into their lives.

I want to acknowledge my debt to the late Daniel Levinson, who mentored me in adult development; to Betty Friedan, whose book *The Fountain Of Age* has funded me as a rich library on aging; and to the reference librarians at the Guilford Free Library, for their unfailing courtesy and resourcefulness.

A Time to Live

Introduction

Often in our fifties and certainly in our sixties we may begin to feel disoriented or dislocated, becoming abruptly, or vaguely, aware of moving through middle age, but still a long way from "old." So where are we? Slipping off the edge, or into the soup, or out of the loop? Something is happening in us and to us that is dislodging us from comfortable roles and routines. Bodily ailments, broken relationships, work changes, or tragic events in the world may contribute to our dis-ease. But something more seismic is going on, difficult to name or understand. We may feel alone in undergoing this anxiety, abnormal, one of the unlucky ones, or that there's something wrong physically or psychologically. *More likely*, we are waking up to our mortality and suffering the birth pangs of passage into another season of the life cycle, the elder season.

A woman in her seventies reflects, "What I remember about that period is that it was a time of tremendous unrest and inner turmoil, similar in many ways to adolescence, in which I felt most of the familiar landmarks shifting, and inside myself a tremendous recklessness and restlessness. I went for some counseling at the time (one of the best things I ever did) and I remember the counselor saying at one point, 'Well, try not to do anything *too* foolish.' I think that period is one in which the unlived life in one presses and asks, 'What are you going to do about me?' "

It may be useful to think of this journey as a period of "elderescence," similar in its peril and promise to earlier periods of adolescence and "middlescence," urgent in its requirement that attention be paid. It's a tricky process we're involved in—one that will yield a more or less successful transition into the elder season. We are struggling to make our own way in the process of creative aging.

While the challenge of creative aging faces us all along the adult life cycle, it becomes pressing as we approach the later years. The good news is that, because of increasing longevity, there *is* an elder season, which may begin around seventy or later, and continue throughout the rest of our lives. Specific age parameters are necessarily imprecise, because the sense of where people are in the age span is shifting and not settled. What matters is to locate one's self within the journey and engage its tasks.

Writers and researchers describe this passage variously. Betty Friedan writes of crossing "the age divide," Daniel Levinson of making "the late adulthood transition," Jane Prétat of "coming to age . . . the croning years and late life transformation," Gail Sheehy of "passage into the Age of Integrity." I choose the phrase *elder passage*. While some may view the term *elder* as male-identified, I intend its use here as gender-inclusive. What matters for both men and women in these years is allowing the underdeveloped or hidden parts of the self to emerge. By doing so we allow ourselves to grow into our full humanity.

I prefer the term *passage* to others, such as *transi-*

tion, because *passage* implies an action of going from one place or condition of being to another. We speak of the "rites of passage," of journeys requiring negotiation and ritualization, of making our own way. We make passages over bodies of water, through notches in mountains. These physical crossings may imprint themselves deeply into our spiritual being, so that what apprehends us outwardly colors and molds the lasting geography of our souls.

We begin to yearn for fulfillment of our life's meaning and to understand that it will only come, if at all, on the way, in finding the promise of the passage. Home is on the road, beyond the horizon, in the next season. *Passage* seems a deep and capacious term for the painful, hopeful pilgrimage of concluding the middle years and moving into the later years. We may be inspired or intimidated by stories of famous older people who made a successful passage and achieved great things in their seventies and eighties. But most of all, we want to live our own deepest hopes for ourselves and the larger community, and do it honestly, passionately, and generously. There is no normative, one-size-fits-all passage. We are not so much looking for models to imitate, as to pool our wisdom in the process of discerning and living our own authentic way. We seek transformation, not just success or survival. As always, change and growth involve painful birthing, and take us into unknown and often fearsome places, where the fresh energy of hope awaits us.

Short-timers attitude

I hope this book will provide companionship, guidance, and encouragement in the living of these years. I have identified seven tasks of creative aging, work to be undertaken if one is to fulfill the promise of the passage. These tasks have emerged out of my struggle to understand and participate in my own passage. They have been tested and shaped with hundreds of others on the same journey, in workshops at Kirkridge Retreat and Study Center, where I was the director for twenty years, and in other venues. In reading the stories of others, one recognizes both the commonality and the uniqueness of one's own story, resonating with its meanings, and gaining strength and insight to live into the integrity of one's own path.

The seven tasks might be described in various ways, but here is how I see them:

1. *Waking Up:* recognizing your own mortality and realizing that now is the time to engage, again, the meaning and direction of your life

2. *Embracing Sorrow:* acknowledging your own losses and griefs and the pain of others, that it may darken and deepen your humanity, yielding compassion

3. *Savoring Blessedness:* remembering and delighting in all the ways you have been, are, and can be a blessed and blessing person in your life

4. *Re-imagining Work:* reviewing and revising the ways in which you want to contribute to society, give your "gift," complete your lifework, live out your purpose in the years ahead

5. *Nurturing Intimacy:* deepening your interconnections with spouse/partner/lover, siblings, children, grandchildren, other family members, friends, nature, yourself, God

6. *Seeking Forgiveness:* doing what you can to clear the decks of your relationships so as to enter the later years with as unburdened a heart as possible

7. *Taking on the Mystery:* accepting life and death, and exploring the ultimate meaning of your life with thanksgiving and hope

At the end of each chapter, I will raise questions around each of the seven tasks, so as to invite the reader to engage particular personal issues. You may find some of the tasks more on-target than others. While these tasks may arise for some early in middle age, and remain vital for the entire aging span, they gain special urgency during this later adulthood transition, as you become freshly aware of the limited and precious time left to live. There is no linear order for these tasks—rather, incentive or stimulus may arise to work on one for a while, then to turn to others, then perhaps months or even years later to return to previous tasks to work some more. I would suggest that you use the tasks not as commandments but as gentle invitations to follow your own path, at your own pace, in your own time. I wish to encourage consciousness and intentionality in making a creative passage.

I use a poem to introduce each chapter, providing a key metaphor for each of the seven tasks. My hope is that the poems may evoke memory and reflection, opening up your capacity for imagination and wonder, and perhaps helping you to access dreams. May they tease out your poetic intuition, providing opportunity for meditation and mulling. I wish to encourage you to pay attention to what rises from the depths of your being, letting the unconscious offer signals, listening to the sonar of the soul.

While this book focuses on the elder passage, it should also be useful to those just waking up to the process of creative aging, as well as those well along in age who may still be engaging some of the tasks, still listening for the song of the soul. Any proposed schema for this period of our lives will be overwhelmed by the sheer multiplicity, diversity, and spontaneity of life itself, which will not tolerate confinement in rational categories. So wherever you are on the aging journey, I hope you will find in this approach useful clues for the living of these years with all your passion and hope.

1. *Waking Up*

The Bustle in a House
The morning after Death
Is solemnest of industries
Enacted upon Earth—

The Sweeping up the Heart,
And putting Love Away
We shall not want to use again
Until Eternity.
                    —Emily Dickinson

Wake-up calls arrive with the innocence of a ringing telephone, but they often come the morning after Death.

My father died in 1981. My siblings and I chose to meet for several days at our parents' retirement home to gather up the loose ends of their lives. Our mother had died the year before, so there were files to sort through, furniture to be assigned, the will to be heard and implemented. We found ourselves sweeping up the heart and hearth of our parents' lives and stirring up the soil of our own.

Because we could not look up to them as an older generation any longer, we looked around and saw each other with newly skinned eyes. Who were we together now that our parents were dead? What did we have as siblings? How were we to accommodate this strange, orphan vulnerability? Death came to visit, and I knew the visitor had come to stay.

I was fifty-five when my father died. I noted the ages of my parents when they died, in their early eighties, and figured, in terms of genetics, how long I might expect to live. I was measuring life no longer from birth, but from death.

The first task of the elder passage is waking up: to the fact that you're in it, that it's coming, or that it's what you've just been through. The death of a parent, spouse, child, or marriage, or the loss of health or job wakes us up to our own mortality. My friend Betty Marsh writes of her anger at involuntary retirement at fifty-five, when the teacher education college where she was employed closed. Two years later she developed breast cancer. "I embarked on a holistic way to manage cancer—by reading cancer research, participating in life history and lifestyle counseling, and nutritional counseling, as well as making my own choices of medical treatment. Dealing with my dreams in one counseling session revealed one 'where I found the lifeless body of a child' and I knew immediately it meant 'the old me is dead.' I accepted this change and went on to sharing leadership in groups dealing with life changes such as loss and illness. I had to ponder the questions, 'What is your purpose in life?' and 'Do you want to get well?' "

A friend in his sixties writes, "It strikes me as I read various books and articles on aging, that in an attempt to balance many negative attitudes toward aging there is a tendency to *oversell* the positive, and in the process there is a loss of honesty about some very common realities. I am constantly aware of the impact of physical limitations and decline even in the most lively and vibrant of my older friends. Because of a bad back I can't chop wood anymore, or play tennis. It's hard to get up off my knees; I have trouble getting in or out of a canoe. I fear physical decline."

Acknowledging fear of our own diminishment and not-so-distant death is an early-warning wake-up call, alerting us to some kind of passage into an unknown and threatening future.

Women encounter menopausal issues, which include loss of reproductive capability, concern about hormonal replacement, fear of osteoporosis, and various threats to one's health and well-being. Some men find their PSA level in the blood rising, and thus need to face the very real possibility of prostate cancer. As one has biopsies and waits to hear whether this latest one is benign or cancerous, one learns to live with a permanent cloud on the horizon. I have been amazed to discover how many personal friends have had prostate cancer and how often it is mentioned as the cause of death in obituaries, which many of us read more frequently than we used to, with the feeling that one of these days it's going to get us, or something else will—and of course it will.

At my forty-fifth college reunion last summer, there was a memorial service for the members of my class, and other classes, who had died since the reunion five years earlier. There were more than six hundred names, some of them known to me. A classmate said that someone had estimated that by the time of our fiftieth reunion, one third of us would have died. That was not, to my knowledge, an actuarial prediction but an anecdotal expression of the fear, along with the delight, we experience as we sweep up the heart at reunions, anniversaries, birthdays, and other regular occasions of celebration and remembrance. Who will be missing the next time we are together?

Body and Soul Wounds

In the months that followed my father's death, as the bustle subsided and the sweeping went on, I felt a heaviness of spirit weighing me down. Surely some of that burden came from my parents' deaths in successive years and the "loss of soul" of which Jungian analyst Marie-Louise von Franz writes. "There is the fear that someone who has died may take the soul of someone close to him along with him into the realm of the dead. . . . 'Loss of soul' appears in the form of the sudden onset of apathy and listlessness; the joy has gone out of life, initiative is crippled, one feels empty, everything seems pointless. Close observation, especially of dreams, will reveal that a large part of the psychic energy has flowed off into the unconscious, and is, therefore, no longer at the disposal of the ego."

But the heaviness I felt within held more than grief over the death of my parents. Fear of nuclear war escalated in the early 1980s. Jonathan Schell, in his book *The Fate of the Earth*, made the distinction between death, which is the end of life, and extinction, which is the end of birth, and noted that the prospect of extinction in a nuclear war gave everyday life a case of coldness, bitterness, despair. Some of us pushed that grief down into the unconscious to anesthetize ourselves from the pain, a process psychiatrist Robert Lifton named "psychic numbing."

It all came in on me one winter day on Long Island six months after my father's death. My wife was conducting a workshop on the island, and I had several hours to kill *(sic)*. I drove to Jones Beach. It was windy and cold. Any place of shelter on the beach? All entrances were fenced off until one appeared with a sign that read: Senior Citizens' Lounge.

There was an open road by the sign leading towards the beach. I thought, I'm fifty-five, a few months from fifty-six, why not? and drove in. I pushed open the swinging door of the lounge and looked around the long room. Couch, chairs, magazines, tables . . . at one of which sat an old gentleman reading a newspaper. We nodded to each other. I feared he might want to talk, but he didn't. Perhaps he felt the same about me. I unpacked my reading materials and journal, and placed a chair near the door, where I could look out a window at the ocean. I leafed through my journal notes of the months since my father's death, watching the waves rolling endlessly upon the shore. Slowly, my tight control of my feelings relaxed, and I felt myself swooning into a strange place of spiritual lethargy, with a loosening of identity and loss of energy.

I was adrift.

I felt ambivalent about life—my life: opaque to my inner self, as though there were layers of insulation around my soul. I was muffled, hidden, under wraps, like Lazarus waiting there in the tomb. I wrote in my journal:

"Only dreams, songs, and poems can help me escape from the dread of death and the fear of life. But my dreams are hidden from me now, my poetry is dried up, and songs sink into sighs. Maybe someday I will once again be like a tree planted by the river, the soil of my soul will loosen, there will be purchase for truth, and I will bring forth fruit in its season. Maybe someday I will see visions and dream dreams, as the prophet promised to young and old, perhaps even to the ambivalent. But not now, not here."

I felt old.

At age sixty-seven the prolific French writer Georges Simenon published a book of diaries titled *When I Was Old*. The diaries had been written ten years before, when Simenon began to *feel* old. He was assailed with self-doubts, wondered if life had any more value for him, if he had any more value for life. Who would miss him when he died? Who would remember him? Then, over a period of several years he made his passage into a most creative and satisfying elder season. The diaries reveal a man needing reassurance that he was still somebody, that he still mattered to people who mattered to him. He wanted his children to know him in his vulnerability and to realize they might become better human beings than he. He found himself feeling, at times, like a stranger in the world.

Brother Georges! Soul brother. I'm not the only one sometimes feeling old at my age.

A woman writes, "I have had a brush with cancer, a breast removed, and some incontinence which I am working to cure. I worry about gaining weight. All of these conditions concern me, but I can't say they make me feel old, balanced against the sheer joy I have in living." Whether we *feel* old or not, we notice the passing of time, and realize we are moving on. In the last of John Updike's books about Rabbit Angstrom, *Rabbit at Rest*, Rabbit retires in his early fifties, goes to Florida, starts the life of pleasure, gets bored with his wife, his leisure, and even his fantasies, and bombs out with a heart attack at age fifty-six. Most of us, in our fifties or sixties, receive some disturbing messages from our aging bodies, messages that give us pause and most likely pain as well. And we learn of friends having strokes, suffering from diabetes, getting cancer or Alzheimer's.

In addition to the wake-up calls of death, loss of soul, and serious illness, there are minor aches and conditions that remind us daily of aging bodies. An annual physical exam revealed that my cholesterol was high. With my wife's help, I moderated my diet. A few months later my cholesterol reading was down to a more tolerable level. What's more, during those months I had lost several pounds, and joy upon joy, two inches around the waist! What a delightful development! I was proud, nay, arrogant. I took seven pairs of pants to the tailor, asking him to take the waist in two inches. My wife suggested I wait on the winter pants and see how things were, "waist-wise," in the fall. But I was not to be denied. My tailor smiled when he saw me, and two months later, after a summer vacation that was disastrous, diet-wise, he smiled again when I brought the winter pants in again to be let out. Nevertheless I had lost one inch that stayed lost. I was, in a most modest way, "fasting," editing my intake, paring down a little.

I have been a moderate walker and swimmer for years, but my back went out one day as I swung a fifty-pound sack of birdseed into its container. Thus I came into the world of chiropractic, learned exercises to strengthen my back and stomach muscles, and accepted the wisdom of not lifting anything over thirty pounds, even if it precluded my carrying a guest's baggage into the house.

How is it with your body and your soul? What wake-up calls are they sending you, alerting you that the rules of the game by which you've played all these years have changed, and attention must be paid?

Turning Sixty

However one is awakened to the shock of one's own aging in the fifties, one is likely to approach the sixtieth birthday as a formidable milestone in the life cycle.

Betty Friedan begins the preface of her massive, rich book *The Fountain of Age* with these words: "When my friends threw a surprise party on my six-tieth birthday, I could have killed them all. Their toasts seemed hostile, . . . pushing me out of . . . the race. Professionally, politically, personally, sexually. . . . I was depressed for weeks after that birthday party, felt removed from them all. I could not face being sixty."

A different approach was taken by my brother Dick, who lives in California, far distant from family members. As his sixtieth birthday drew near, he decided to invite a number of friends and their families to help him celebrate. Over a hundred people gathered in a church fellowship hall: students from his teaching years, members of several singing groups to which he belonged, members of his men's group, hiking comrades, teaching colleagues. Some friends made up a bluegrass band, and there was singing and dancing through the evening.

Dick writes: "So my life for the last twenty years in the Bay Area was basically there. Some have written me saying that they want to give themselves that kind of party in their future. I am sort of amazed that I thought to do this, and then did it. . . . The truly best part of this all is that I see many of these friends regularly in my life, so I have my birthday with me the year round."

Dick ritualized his sixtieth birthday and made a party of the passage.

My own sixtieth was a modest affair. My wife wrote family and friends, inviting them to remember me with a card or note, and we celebrated the occasion with a small group of close friends and neighbors. One gift was a homemade card, on the outside of which, in large letters, were the words "A STAR WAS BORN." On the inside several small stars surrounded a huge star in the center. The little stars had names: "joker," "dog daddy," "cook?", "stud preacher," "bird man," and so forth. The big star was named "FRIEND." I was touched that the senders of the card had experienced me primarily as a friend. While I had invested heavily over the years in being a husband, father, stepfather, minister, and colleague, I had not given friendship much attention. Strange to realize, at my age, that I am a rookie at friendship. I am waking up to the fact that I want and need friends in these years, and that it will require more energy and care from me than I have been able or willing to give in the past.

One surprise was a lovely birthday letter from my brother John. There had long been respect and affection between us, but there was also an emotional reticence, which we could break through only once in a while, late at night, after a few drinks. Now, out of nowhere, it seemed, came this two-and-a-half-page, single-spaced, handwritten letter, recalling my being his older brother who could do things he couldn't do as we were growing up, and our losing track of each other as we pursued our schooling and took up professional and family lives. And then:

How strange, years later, to find ourselves near each other in Pennsylvania. There were Thanksgiving dinners and New Year's Eve parties, and kids all around and snow and play and talk. Yes, now there was much more talking. It was, for me, as if our relationship had at last come fully grown. We talked and talked on those visits. You were still "older brother," but my being a "younger brother" didn't mean what it had for those many years before. Strange how long it can take to grow up into a relationship. And so we have traveled these past ten years, through kids growing up and Mom and Dad's dying. We've hung around each other all these years, you and I. I look back now and, suddenly, I am very glad for that. Who would I have been without you? An older brother and a

pal you've been. How much more lonely it would
have been without you out there!

> Thanks and Love,
> your brother
> John

What a gift John gave me by so generously
remembering our brotherhood over the years and
evoking my own memories of our relationship. It *is*
less lonely out there because of John and Dick and my
sister, Rose. It matters when we and our children
drive or fly long distances to be with one another in
times of family sorrow and joy. While mingled feelings
of parental favoritism, ancient rivalries, or wounded
histories may abide, sisters and brothers are still bound
by blood and family heritage in relationships capable of
recovery and healing. A woman writes, "My only
brother died last year. I have no sisters. I feel a loneliness now from the realization that, with my parents'
deaths years ago, there is no one who knew me when
I was a child, none to help me remember my early
years."

When a sibling is "lost" to you, part of your own
life is lost. Especially in the years since our parents'
deaths my siblings and I have paid fresh attention to
one another, wanting, I think, to live our brotherhood
and sisterhood as deeply as we can, while we can.

My best sixtieth birthday gift arrived a few days
after the day itself. I had written a letter to my second
daughter, Barbara, on the occasion of her thirtieth
birthday two weeks before. When she and her siblings were growing up, I was unaware of the ways
in which birth order affected one's development and

relationships. Barb and I had gotten stuck in some destructive behavior patterns, and over the years I came to realize it was mostly my fault, in the context of a family system that had its share of dysfunction. The advent of her thirtieth and my sixtieth birthdays woke me up to the realization that I wanted to take some initiative to try to clear things up between us, and that we didn't have forever to do it. So I wrote her, asking forgiveness for all the ways, known and unknown, that I had hurt her and damaged her life. I was asking for a general amnesty.

Barb responded with a letter dated on my birthday. She wrote, in part: "Your letter brought tears to my eyes—reading your thoughts of the thirty years we have experienced each other. I too believe there is a lot of love between us, and I think our relationship is stronger and more natural with all the work we have done. . . . Life is too short to carry all that baggage of anger and rejection around. I do forgive you."

I read those last words over and over. They took a stone off my heart. I felt tremendous relief and gratitude. Barb set us both free to live gladly into our future as father and daughter, and adult friends. We still have our issues but have learned how to draw back from the edge, and there is a mutually blessed assurance that our bond is strong, tender, and enduring.

It is both a simple and a difficult matter that in the relationships that mean the most to us, we are absolutely dependent upon one another for forgiveness. There is no other way out of a burdened past than to grant appropriate penitence and restitution. A birthday, anniversary, or holiday may offer a wake-up call, provide an "excuse" to reach out to someone, and invite us once again into the holy healing process of sweeping up the heart.

Around my sixtieth birthday I began waking up to the realization that life, all life, *my* life is sheer gift. Without advance notice, feelings of thanksgiving would occasionally wash over self-satisfaction or self-pity.

A friend sent me a translation of a poem by the thirteenth-century Persian poet Rumi:

> For sixty years I have been forgetful,
> every minute, but not for a second
> has this flowing toward me stopped or slowed.
> I deserve nothing. Today I recognize
> that I am the guest the mystics talk about.
> I play this living music for my Host.
> Everything today is for the Host.

Yes! The sun shines and rain falls on us without reference to our virtue, performance, or faith. Gratitude began to grow in me. I found myself, sometimes, less defensive, more willing to initiate peacemaking where that seemed appropriate. I began to notice the fragrance of lilacs in May, to hear the gorgeous cacophony of birdsong at dawn, to look and look at the outrageous colors of autumn, to savor the taste of morning coffee and evening wine. My senses were waking up.

★   ★   ★

And then something happened in my life that took me to a new level of delight.

Becoming a Grandparent

If many wake-up calls come the morning after death, some come the morning after birth. In the early spring of 1987 I learned that my eldest daughter, Cathy, was pregnant with her first child. I began praying for Cathy, her husband, Mike, and the "question-person" beginning its journey in her womb. As the months went on, I became aware of my deepening investment in that nascent life and noticed a tendering of the already deep bond between Cathy and me as daughter and father. Something was being born between us as well.

That May I saw other parents-to-be busily at work on a high branch of the tall oak down the hill from our house. The brilliant orange-and-black Baltimore oriole male and his olive-yellow partner were flying in and out of that tree with grasses and twigs in their beaks, stitching together a nest. A brave nest, it hung down nearly a foot below the branch, a deep, pendant, oval cradle, swinging, sometimes wildly, in the wind. The soon-to-be-born are vulnerable, their nests fragile, new life precarious.

Katie, my first grandchild, was born on July 2. Mother and baby well. Hurray! Joy! Willy-nilly, I had become an elder in my family. A rookie elder. Whether a wise or foolish one was not, is not yet, known. By definition a rookie is a beginner, with no guarantee of lasting the season, much less making it for good. Katie's presence in the world caused me to begin wondering what it might mean for me to become a good elder in my family, work, society. It was such delight to see Katie—photos of her first days of life, then to see her and touch her and hold her in my arms, and, a few months later, baptize her. There was comfort in this new generation in the family and world, life going on, a kind of wonderment mixed with thanksgiving. There was also a new sense of responsibility on my part. How might I be a good grandparent? How might I nourish and encourage and care for this child, and indeed care for all the children being born into the world, one fourth of whom in this country are born, blameless and innocent, into poverty, and most of whom will never get out of it?

I found myself wondering whether Katie's birth might signal a new birthing of my own. I was sixty-one.

Do you have grandchildren or nieces or nephews, or other young ones who look to you for wisdom and support?

For some of us, grandparenting is a mixed bag. A woman wrote me: "I have one son who has hurt my feelings over and over again. He lives only a little over an hour away, but I see him and his family only three times a year. I wish that I could have had an active part in his children's growing up, but I don't. It isn't intentional on my son's part, but it still hurts. On the other hand, I have a wonderful relationship with my other son's son, who is my oldest grandchild. I took care of him a whole month when his parents went to Europe one year. I took him to his soccer games and cooked meals he liked. He says he thinks we bonded during that month. He was born the day after my fiftieth birthday. I called him on his tenth birthday and asked him how it felt. He said, 'I'd rather be ten than sixty.' "

Though my life was brighter because Katie was in it, there was still a heaviness within me. I was more anxious than curious, more conscious of losses than gains. Though my work was productive, I was sometimes bored ... depressed? Now and then in the middle of the afternoon I would look out my office window and wonder what I was still doing there in that job. I felt the limits of my life, the smallness of scale of my efforts, the seeming insignificance of my days. I was aware of Erik Erikson's thesis that the central psychological and spiritual struggle of middle age is the tension between generativity and stagnation. And I understood, in my head, that the only way to generativity is *through* experiences of stagnation, and that there are, inevitably, aspects of self-absorption in the midst of arguably generative periods of our lives. What I didn't yet believe or imagine was that what may appear as hopelessly barren and joyless periods have within them the seeds of rebirth. What appears to be fruitless time may in fact be fallow time. What seems like years of wasted life may not have been wasted at all, but in ways not yet known, necessary to growth into one's full humanity.

Significant Dreams

In fact, my soul was getting ready to send me another wake-up call.

On the night of February 28, 1990, I had two back-to-back dreams. In the first dream, I am in our house at Kirkridge. I stand looking out the kitchen window at the back of the house, facing west. The sliding glass doors on the front of the house are (in the dream) now on the back, on the west side. Several young men in blue jeans are milling around just outside the window in the driveway. They are moving towards me, evidently intent on coming into the house. I am scared and frantically try to lock the sliding doors. But I can't do it in time. They crowd in and around me.

I woke up, disturbed but relieved to find that I was "just" dreaming.

I went back to sleep and dreamed a second time. I have returned to speak at a church where I had been the pastor. I look out at the congregation and see many familiar faces. Suddenly I realize I have left my Bible and speaking notes behind, where I am housed, and the service is about to begin. I am frustrated and anxious, wondering how to wing it, when a woman, whose face is in the shadows and who is unknown to me, offers to drive me to the place where I am staying, to retrieve my material. I woke up troubled and curious.

The next morning I wrote down my still-vivid memories of the two dreams, related them to my wife, and began pondering their meanings. In the first dream, what in me is feeling threatened? Who or what is trying to invade me or take me over or join me? The night before we had watched a video, a story about young pilots in World War II, training for missions off carriers in the Pacific. Lots of young, strong male energy. Is my ego trying to keep this young male energy out of the house of my soul, fearful of the disorder to come? In the dream I am *facing west*, looking towards sunset. Maybe the seemingly "hostile" young male energy isn't hostile at all but wants to come in and rejuvenate my soul. I can't keep these young men out anyway, so I might as well let them take me over with their irresistible strength and confidence.

In terms of Jungian psychology, the major polarity to be engaged at each transition period in adult development is the Young/Old polarity. Here I was at age sixty-three, in the midst of the elder passage. The youngster (Puer) and the oldster (Senex) were struggling in me towards a fresh integration and a new balance. Senex had been reigning for some time, pulling at me with feelings of ambivalence, stagnation, spiritual lethargy. Now Puer wanted his day. I thought I had lost my archetypal hero long ago, but here came those young blue-jeaned heroes insisting on energizing the elder being born in me. Is there such a thing as a heroic elder? Is there a possibility of transformation in this transition? Might there be some kind of sunrise in the context of this sunset? I took comfort in the fact that, in the dream, the fresh energy was already overwhelming my futile defenses. I couldn't prevent it, nor could I have engineered it. Something powerful was happening in me and to me.

I have had the second dream many times in many versions. It has to do with performance anxiety without adequate preparation or resources. In this dream, back-to-back with the first, in what specific ways am I feeling bereft of the tools of my trade at this time in my life? How do I feel ill-equipped or disabled for the task at hand? And what is the particular lateness of the hour? Might it represent the sense that time is running out for my writing and other things I want to do? Is the shadowy female figure, in Jungian terms, my anima ready to help me retrieve my resources so that I can do my job properly? If so, my resources are waiting in my files and my memory. It is not too late for retrieval, but it is time to begin imagining the acts of retrieval.

I was excited and encouraged, first, that I remembered these two dreams—not a common experience for me—and, second, that the dreams came back-to-back the same night. They literally woke me up with the good news that my inner self (or the Spirit) had not given up on me. Dreams can be carriers of identity or vocation. I think the first dream portrayed the house of my soul: it was a dream of identity and being. The second dream portrayed the work of my soul: it was a dream of vocation and doing. Together, they awakened me to the fresh energy "flowing towards me," within me.

In a developmental transition such as the elder passage, one may be freshly vulnerable to dreams, poetry or music, or natural beauty. External events can dislodge the obsolete order of one's life, loosening the Lazarus-like bindings around the soul. The right brain gains prominence, yielding apprehensions or initiatives other than those of the conscious ego. You may remember one or several especially vivid dreams that turn out to be paradigmatic for your journey.

We do well, in transition time, to pay attention to whatever is strange, whatever breaks routine, custom or convention, whatever takes us by surprise. Wake-up calls come in many guises, raising questions. One looks and listens for clues from the unconscious in order to get one's bearings in the elder passage.

Retirement Issues

We also begin to face retirement. We may dread it, long for it, be relieved by it, feel we did it too soon, or be enjoying it. Maybe we were or will be forced into early retirement or have the option of continuing the work we've been doing for decades, as long as health and opportunity permit.

But, in some degree, many of us fear retirement. We notice that some people, mainly men, retire like Rabbit Angstrom and die. We fear being "put out to pasture" by society, if not our family too, being affectionately tolerated but not expected to contribute much anymore. We fear that nobody will know who we are if we move to a different place to live. We wonder how to create significant connections to the world when the work connection so vital to our identity and visibility is lost. Who will we be when we're no longer practicing our trade the way we always did? (These are issues that I will explore in more detail in Chapter 4.)

Then there is the fear that financial resources in retirement will not be sufficient to sustain the standard of living, however affluent or modest, to which we've become accustomed. We may believe in simplifying our lifestyle, but wonder whether there will be enough money to be comfortable and secure. I found myself in recent years worrying a lot about these things.

The next chapter of my elder passage came into view when my wife and I decided to retire from Kirkridge. The decision was made in late 1992, and it released me to imagine an ending time, and to begin to see the shape of our twenty years at Kirkridge.

Relief flooded in. How lovely it would be not to have to worry any longer about the well-being of a cherished enterprise. What would it be like to have weekends free? Where would we choose to live? I was excited and delighted with these imaginings and readier to be on my way than I had anticipated. The young men in my dream were definitely occupying the house of my soul.

The year before, I had grudgingly acknowledged my sixty-fifth birthday, having made my ragged way through the previous year humming the Beatles' classic "When I'm Sixty-Four." (How did those young men understand our fear at not being needed when we get older?) Two weeks after this birthday I received in the mail an envelope from the government in which there was . . . a Medicare card! I felt personally offended. How had they found me? I hadn't asked for this. It was as though they had told me, "Buddy, you are certifiably old, and here's the card to prove it." Well, I must have applied for it months before and forgotten all about it. Of course I was glad to have the coverage, but it was a painful birthday for me, and I wanted to get through it without any fuss. At sixty I could anticipate life going on for many years *as it had been*. At sixty-five I knew things were beginning to change and would never again be the same. So it was a comfort to realize that something new was being born in me, that the elder season was at hand, and that the time was ripe and right to leave the old and enter the new with fresh energy and hope. By the time of my actual retirement, I was sixty-eight.

Jungian analyst Clarissa Pinkola Estes, author of *Women Who Run with the Wolves*, tells the story of four old women in her foster family who taught her about the glorious power of age. She calls them the "Dancing Grandmas," referring to a custom in that immigrant family: when a daughter is betrothed, the old women attempt to "kill" the groom. They try to dance him to death, wearing him down until they finally agree he has passed the test. "The dancing old women gave [everyone present] a yearning to be old enough to gain *that* kind of power, old enough to have that vivid play, old enough to take such joy from watching, teaching, testing the young, counseling the middle-aged, and yes, even burying the dead whom they had loved hard all their lives. . . . The grandmas taught that becoming an elder does not occur simply by living many years but more so by what we and fate fill us with over those years. And that it is never to late to deepen. We can prepare *now* for that crossing into the power of age."

Now is the time to cross over into the power of our age and to sweep up the heart and hearth of our lives thus far. We begin by acknowledging our sorrow.

Questions for pondering:

What wake-up calls is your body or soul sending you?

What death events or births got your attention?

When did you last weep?

❋

2. Embracing Sorrow

What is sorrow for? It is a storehouse set
On Rocks for wheat, barley, corn, and tears.
One steps to the door on a round stone.
The storehouse feeds all the birds of sorrow.
And I say to myself: Will you have
Sorrow at last? Go on, be cheerful in autumn,
Be stoic, yes, be tranquil, calm,
Or, in the valley of sorrows spread your wings.
—Robert Bly

Robert Bly's poem provides rich images for finding our way, step by step, into our own sorrow and that of others. I invite you to linger with these words: exploring the geography of your own life-wounds, engaging in dialogue with your soul, and preparing to hear the sorrow stories of others. These steps constitute the second task of the elder passage: embracing sorrow.

What is sorrow for? It is a storehouse set
On Rocks for wheat, barely, corn, and tears.

The storehouse is a common granary for all our losses, pain, fear, despair, loneliness. Pain is a specific hurt; sadness is a condition of being in low spirits; grief is deep anguish. All are poured into sorrow, a generous repository where nourishment and healing may be found. As we grieve our losses and suffer our heartache, sorrow may darken and enrich our life, and in some way not yet understood, disallow self-pity, make our fate acceptable, and increase our compassion for others.

One steps to the door on a round stone.

The act of taking the first step is a decision to take personal responsibility for engaging your own sorrow, in the realization that nobody else can do it for you. The door, the threshold, is a liminal place of vulnerability and possibility. In the fifth chapter of the Gospel of John, Jesus asks a question of one who has been an invalid for thirty-eight years: "Do you want to be healed?" Wouldn't anybody want healing, liberation after all those years—wouldn't you or I? Yet there's a key question for us: do you *want* to deal with your sorrow? Jesus' response to the invalid's excuse as to why he couldn't initiate his healing was an invitation: "Take up your pallet, and walk." The invalid did so, acting upon the confidence inspired in him, and discovering resources within himself to take the first step towards healing. Some of us have been, or felt, invalid or invalidated for longer than thirty-eight years. We may be ready, at our age, to accept an invitation to step up to the door of the storehouse named sorrow.

There is also a communal character to taking the first step. When we tell our own sorrow stories to ourselves and others, and when we hear the sorrow stories of others, we are moving out of private grief into public sorrow. The *round* stone reminds us that, in this chapter, we are entering a community in which we and others make ourselves visible, audible, vulnerable, accessible. Sorrow is the great circle of mutual accessibility, a community where there is safety, comfort, and acceptance. William Blake writes, "Joy and woe are woven fine, a clothing for the Soul divine." Now is the time to reweave our years, inspecting and accepting the new texture with all its dark, gorgeous, and tear-stained threads, a cloth woven fine out of the rough material of our life. Now is the time to enter the storehouse.

The storehouse feeds all the birds of sorrow.

It relieves as well as pains us to name the varieties of sorrow that mark our lives. As some people touch or make rubbings of the name of a loved one on the Vietnam Veterans Memorial wall, we, by touching and naming the sore places in our lives, may find some comfort and healing. We might be surprised to discover that our souls are being nourished and strengthened in this storytelling.

Now we can taste our family's sorrow, the various genetic faults passed down from generation to generation: predisposition to cancer, heart trouble, alcoholism, depression. We can note the failures of each generation: our parents' unfulfilled dreams, their neuroses, their wounds imprinted in our soul and body along with their love for us, their abandonments as well as their nourishing of our hopes—all the broken, yearning ways they impacted our life.

Now we can acknowledge some of our own faults, those fissures of betrayal, hurt, or turning away that tore relationships and may, by some strange grace, make us able now to turn back again. I recall my father's desire to talk politics and theology in his later years, and how I found ways to postpone such talks because I needed space from him, or so I thought. Now I regret not listening when I had the chance, not offering that small gift to my father, and depriving myself of conversations to remember and savor.

My mother kept her secrets within, disappointment and resignation visible in her eyes. It seemed to me that she had depths of unlived life within her, but I never came to know her inner truth. It saddens me that her soul, like her face, is now hidden from me in shadowy mystery. Both my parents died quickly of a stroke and a heart attack, so there was no opportunity to process these things together.

We can remember our experience of giving and receiving damage in the family. Whom have you cursed as well as blessed? Whose growth have you stunted? Towards whom do you feel grievance or guilt, that you are victim or villain? Contrition is part of sorrow, and it is important to move towards greater self-knowledge and self-responsibility if one wants to clear one's soul and grow into mature humanity.

We also bear a historical sorrow. Lawrence Langer, in his book *Holocaust Testimonies: The Ruins of Memory*, tells the stories of three hundred Jewish survivors of the Holocaust. He notes that at times they speak from "common memory," in a chronological, ordered, composed manner, and at other times, from "deep memory," reliving their horrible experiences with a surge of the original pain, chaos, and sense of irretrievable loss. Langer observes the fear of survivors that the very story they try to tell drives off the audience they seek to capture.

So we too fear that others will not believe or

understand what really happened to us, whether it seems ordinary and unworthy of recounting, or shameful and unsafe to recount, or too horrible and painful to recount or even remember. Survivors of child abuse, whether physical, emotional, or sexual, may suffer eruptions of deep memory in fearful flash-backs, or be ambushed by ancient terrors triggered by an external event or inner revelation. When that happens the unhealed chaos pours out, overwhelming dikes that had stood for decades.

We carry the sorrow of neighbors, friends, fellow pilgrims. The grief of people special to us may make our soul porous and so give us access to our own grief, or it may cause us to harden our heart to anesthetize the pain.

We behold the sorrows of the world, unbidden, on the evening news: massacres; the flight of refugees; ethnic cleansing; famine; pollution; bombings; children killing children; violent incidents of anti-Semitism, homophobia, racism; and the despairing rage of young black males in our country. We sense, as through glass, the distant ache of the mothers and fathers of the forty thousand children who die every day in this world of hunger or preventable disease. Poet Adrienne Rich gathers up our aching litanies in her words: "My heart is moved by all I cannot save: / so much has been destroyed."

Each sorrow that we allow to touch our heart takes us into the sorrow of God. Who can fathom the bottomless, endless sorrow of God?

Yet the storehouse of sorrow is a rich resource of nourishment and healing, as we shall see. Sorrow shared may yield a feast of memory and hope. There may be a communion of comfort, as there often is at the Vietnam Veterans Memorial and other such wailing walls. The apostle Paul said that the Spirit searches our hearts with groans too deep for words. Our groaning for our own little ones, and the AIDS babies, and all the slaughtered innocents echoes the groaning of God, as deep calls to deep.

And I say to myself: Will you have
Sorrow at last?

I knew little of sorrow for forty years and more. I was the eldest son in a family where, according to my siblings, I received more affirmation and encouragement than I deserved or than came their way. For decades I was cheerful, positive, unacquainted with my shadow, unconscious of the woundedness of our family system and thus of my own wounds. Entering the ministry, I found myself in a role where it was my task to comfort others in their sorrow, while denying or hiding any sorrow of my own.

Then my first wife, Peg, and I divorced in 1974. There followed years of grief and loss, for her, for me, for our four children. Our original family unit was broken. I resigned from my church and had to move five hundred miles away to find a job. I suffered the sadness of not being able to live in the same house with my teenage daughters and eight-year-old son, seeing them a few times a year instead of every day. It was, and is to this day, the most painful loss I have suffered in my life. I discovered I had relationships with four separate individuals who happened to be my children, rather than being just the father of a family. But each of us worked hard over many years to foster our relationships and find new ways as adults to relate to one another. Eventually, I felt blessed, thankful, and, to a large degree, healed.

Early on I remarried. It is a joyous marriage, not without contention but providing intimacy, comfort, delight, and much laughter.

Then, one August day came a phone call to one of my daughters at our summer cottage. Her mother had been diagnosed with the worst kind of brain tumor, with perhaps a year to live. I saw my daughter receiving this news at the phone like hammer blows to the head, crying out in horror. In the months that followed, I watched my children rearrange their lives to spend time with their mother, doing their grief work with her and among themselves along the way. They all knew, and Peg knew, that she would not be present at our son Bob's forthcoming wedding or ever know his children.

Peg and I had been cordial with each other across the years since the divorce. We "did well" at graduations, weddings, and other public occasions. We were courteous and even friendly on the phone or in person picking up or dropping off one of our children. But we had never chosen to work through the painful process of our parting, and now it was too late. So, how to express my own sorrow to her? I felt like an awkward bystander, which I was. I was advised to write, as phone calls and visits became increasingly unsatifying modes of communicating with her. So I wrote her, expressing my gratitude for our years together, my delight in our children and grand-children, asking forgiveness for much, honoring that season of our lives we shared. I didn't expect to receive a letter from her, nor did I receive one, but I felt connected in spirit to her and participating, even in this small way, with her in her fight for life. Now all those twenty-three years have gone down into eternity shrouded in silence.

There is an underground river that flows deeper than remorse through the bottomlands of our lives into the valley of sorrow, carrying our tears toward the ocean. And some of us are left with wounds un-healed, loves unrequited, understanding not achieved.

Peg's dying and death caused each of the children, in their own ways, to remember their grief and loss at the time of the divorce, the time of their father's departure. My thirty-two-year-old daughter Nancy told me that fall that she was meeting with a grief group weekly, receiving the surge and mix of feelings arising out of her "deep memory." Several months later I received a long letter from her in which she spoke of being abandoned by me when I left home. She was fourteen at the time. She spoke of her spirit being broken by the divorce and my departure, of her loss of trust in me. She affirmed her love for me but said we would need to forge a new relationship based on who and where she was now as a person. It was painful for me to read and reread her letter, realizing afresh how much confusion and anguish the divorce had caused Nancy and others. I wrote her, acknowl-edging her continuing pain and accepting her word that we would need to evolve a fresh relationship out of the old.

In the months that followed we exchanged addi-tional letters, and then one day on a long walk together in the woods we shared tears and found a healing closure. While acknowledging that the fourteen-year-old girl *felt* abandoned, I could hope that in time the thirty-two-year-old woman would understand that I had not abandoned her or her siblings, that nothing in this world could ever bring me to do so.

One begins to understand that some part of one's sorrow will always be there deep in the soul, darkening and enriching that space, and that from time to time there will come a surge of chaos, loss, and grief from deep memory, circling round in our life and the lives of those dear to us. The time of sweeping up the heart will be upon us once again, a time for doing more chaos work, letting more tears out and healing in. Yes, you and I will have sorrow at last, though we may deny it as long as we can.

> *Go on, be cheerful in autumn,*
> *Be stoic, yes, be tranquil, calm,*

In Anne Tyler's novel *Saint Maybe*, Doug Bedloe, retired in his mid-sixties, and his wife, Bee, are driving home from a picnic with their son Ian. Their older son, Danny, had been killed a few years before in an automobile accident that might have been suicidal. Bee starts talking about Danny and says,

> "Sometimes I have the strangest feeling. I give this start and I think, 'Why!' I think, 'Why, here we are! Just going about our business the same as usual!' And yet so much has changed. Danny is gone—our golden boy, our first baby boy that we were so proud of . . . and our lives have turned so makeshift and second class, so second string, so second fiddle, and everything's been lost. Isn't it

amazing that we keep on going? That we keep . . . getting hungry and laughing at jokes on TV? When our oldest son is dead and gone, and we'll never see him again, and our life's in ruins!"

"Now, sweetie," he said.

"We've had such extraordinary troubles," she said, "and somehow they've turned us ordinary. That's what's so hard to figure. We're not a special family anymore."

"Why, sweetie, of course we're special,"
he said.

"We've turned uncertain. We've turned into worriers."

"Bee, sweetie."

"Isn't it amazing?"

It was astounding, if he thought about it. But he was careful not to.

No wonder we're careful not to think about it. It is painful to realize that our family is special only to its own members, and that most people have extraordinary troubles. Yes, there are ruins in everyone's life, and no one is immune from feelings of having to settle for some kind of second class. But finally it is a kind of comfort and relief to know that we are ordinary people in the human family—uncommon common people especially loved by God. After a time of vainly trying to anesthetize our pain, we may be ready to enter our sorrow.

Or, in the valley of sorrows spread your wings.

In the stories that follow, stories of people who in

various ways embraced their sorrow, you may recognize something of your own experience or possibility.

Every summer on vacation in Michigan I would see my friend Barbara. Our parents had cottages on the same hillside overlooking a lake. We shared a common dock with another family on the hill and almost daily gathered to exchange the gossip of the lake and the stories of our lives. Barbara married Bob Harris; I married Peg. Sue Harris was born, as was my daughter Cathy. They were fourteen when Sue developed cancer of the jaw. After three years of pain and disfigurement, she died. Barbara and Bob were divorcing, and there was little communication between them. It seems that after Sue was cremated, there was uncertainty as to where to put her ashes, so they had been left in an urn at the funeral home— where they stayed for nineteen years! Then, one summer Bill Harris, Sue's younger brother, persuaded his mother and father to join him at the lake they all loved for a simple ritual. They asked me to accompany them, and we went out on the lake in their boat, talked of Sue, listened to a psalm and a prayer. The three of them took handfuls of Sue's ashes from a container and scattered them on the waters of the lake, and we returned to shore, teary-eyed, eased, peaceful. After all those years, Barbara and Bob became able and willing—with a little help from Bill—to spread their wings in that particular valley of their sorrow.

Hap and Dorothy were married in 1967. Barely a month later he was sent to Vietnam, a twenty-two-year-old believing in the justice of the United States' waging of the war. He became a secret agent, disappeared into Vietnamese society, witnessing events he was unable to tell anyone about. Meanwhile Dorothy had decided the war was unjust. After Hap was out of the Army, she participated in the protests to end the war. Hap was angry and felt humiliated when he witnessed her anti-war activity, and he told her so. But they were never able to discuss it further. They "stuffed" it from then on, letting it affect and infect their relationship. They experienced some healing, and more silence. In the fall of 1990 they participated in a retreat at Kirkridge for Vietnam vets and their families, where, together with others, they found their way to re-enter their long sorrow. A few weeks after the retreat I received a Christmas card from them in which Dorothy wrote, "The healing is too deep and wordless to discuss. You will appreciate, Bob, what it means that twenty-one years after Hap felt humiliated by my participation in the War Moratorium, we walked together in December with the Friends in Quakertown, one hundred and twenty strong, marching for a peaceful solution of the Gulf crisis."

Sometimes one comes through harrowing experiences of loss into a strange new kind of freedom. A seventy-four-year-old woman writes, "I have lost my parents, husband, and many friends. At each death I cried, picked up the pieces, and went on. However, discovering I am no longer anyone's daughter or wife or mother (middle-aged children don't need mothering) has led me to find out who I am. And for the first time in my life I am totally free to do as I damn please, make my own mistakes without worrying about what people will say. Growing up I guess."

Thomas Stoddard is a gay attorney in his late forties. For years he headed the Lambda Legal Defense

Educational Fund, a gay and lesbian legal rights group, mentoring other gay and lesbian attorneys working on behalf of the gay community, especially those suffering from AIDS. Some years ago he learned he himself had AIDS, and he found himself nursing the same wounds, taking the same medications, and haunted by the same fears as his clients. He writes, "I became the client as well as the lawyer." But instead of dragging him down, the disease "crystalized, purified" his work. "My most effective antiviral drug is political commitment, because it gets me so worked up. . . . I wouldn't wish this experience on anyone, but I find it absolutely fascinating. . . . I'm very glad to be living this. . . . I feel as though I'm on a precipice. I worry that I might fall, but my perspective is now broader and deeper. I see an all-encompassing vista, one that connects the past to the future, one that ties me to all other people who have suffered." Thomas Stoddard, his life foreshortened by AIDS, fueled by an early and urgent wisdom, is nourishing his people, seeking to make this country safe and just for its gay, lesbian, and bisexual citizens. Like many others he is an elder before his time, spreading his wings in the valley of sorrow.

When David Dodson Gray's mother, suffering from Alzheimer's, entered a nursing home, he began writing distant family members about his daily visits with her. Those letters told of the unfolding character of her disease, his own emotional and spiritual turmoil, and his struggles to find new skills to sustain their communicating to the last. David fed her and told her the latest family stories and political events. He describes learning how to "listen to garble," and more difficult, how to "speak to garble." When showing his mother old family photographs, he became aware of his own "need to remember, and . . . interest in pondering this amazing process of recollection . . . by which the past is so wonderfully retrieved." One evening, he writes, while sitting with his mother, "I suddenly connected with all the times I sat with [my] children while they were going to bed. I told Mom about how Liz and I sang our children lullabies. Then I started singing softly to my mother all the lullabies I could remember."

After his mother's death two and a half years later, David put his letters together in the form of a book, *I Want to Remember: A Son's Reflection on His Mother's Alzheimer Journey.* One sees a son in his mid-sixties and a mother in her early eighties both struggling to maintain their fading ability to communicate. "There is much I regret about the disease and what a wasting it was of her in those years, but I am grateful too for the use we made of that time, salvaging so much even while we both were losing so much." David speaks finally of a "soft sorrow that recedes when I am caught up in other activities or relationships but which is always there." Here is a son practicing a clear-eyed, tender fidelity to his mother, finding nourishment for himself and others in a storehouse named sorrow.

What has it meant, what might it mean, for you to spread your wings in the valley of sorrow? Is it possible, as the prophet Isaiah wrote, "they who wait for the Lord shall renew their strength, they shall mount up with wings like eagles, they shall run and not be weary, they shall walk and not faint"?

There is a stewardship of sorrow, tending it, attending to it, not wallowing but conserving, that its dark food may remain available to nourish ourselves and others. A fifty-seven-year-old woman writes: "My deepest loss is a divorce after thirty years of marriage, a divorce which I initiated. Almost more than the divorce, I grieved selling the house in which we had been a family for twenty years. I called my children to join me in saying 'good-bye' to the house. I have contact with the people who bought my home and know that a new baby sleeps in the room that was mine before the marriage ended. Somehow it comforts me to think of new life coming out of the old. Recently I found a billfold-size picture of my husband and me at our wedding and put it out on a table. I grieved by facing what I had to do. During the long divorce process I was a part-time Hospice chaplain. I remember just sitting and being present to my sadness. I called it 'chaplaining' my grief. Recently as I sat with a member of my congregation who had just lost her husband of forty-nine years, she said, 'I believe what you tell me because I know you have suffered painful losses and come through to the other side.' "

Whence comes this generosity of spirit that sometimes flowers in adversity, this magnanimity born of diminishment? Aeschylus wrote, "Drop, drop—in our sleep, upon the heart / Sorrow falls, memory's pain, / And to us, though against our very will, / Even in our own despite, / Comes wisdom / By the awful grace of God."

One day in May 1992, in the beginning months of the Bosnian war, Serbian mortar fire raining down on the besieged city of Sarajevo struck a line of people waiting to buy bread in a bakery, killing twenty-two persons. The next afternoon at four, Vedran Smailovic, a cellist in the Sarajevo Opera, came with a chair and his cello to that cobblestone street in front of the bakery. Risking his life in the face of continuing artillery and sniper fire, Smailovic, dressed in formal black suit and white tie, played at four p.m. every day for twenty-two days the majestic and sorrowful lines of Albinoni's "Adagio," honoring each person who had perished. He wasn't able to stop the war or prevent its coming horrors, but he did what he could, playing a requiem for the living and dead, embracing the sorrow of Sarejevo and of the world, embracing his own.

In 1985 William Styron, then sixty years old, was struck with a clinical depression so severe it drove him to the brink of suicide. In his book *Darkness Visible*, he describes his daily despair, beginning with a "merciless drumming" in his head, an acute sense of loss, a dread of abandonment, a fogbound horror without hope. He suffered through fruitless therapies, and made plans to kill himself. One night, as he watched a tape of an old movie whose scene was a music conservatory, there "came a contralto voice, a sudden soaring passage from the Brahms Alto Rhapsody. This sound . . . pierced my heart like a dagger, and in a flood of swift recollection I thought of all the joys the house had known: the children who had rushed through its rooms, the festivals, the love and work, the honestly earned slumber, the voices and nimble commotion, the perennial tribe of cats and dogs and birds. . . . All this I realized was more than I could ever abandon." He woke his wife; she took him to the hospital, where, during weeks of seclusion, his healing began.

Time and solitude became, for him, the sanctuary of healing. Later he agreed that there were genetic roots to his depression. "But I'm persuaded that an even more significant factor was the death of my mother when I was thirteen; this disorder and early sorrow—the death or disappearance of a parent, especially a mother, before or during puberty—appears repeatedly in the literature of depression as a trauma sometimes likely to create nearly irreparable emotional havoc. The danger is especially apparent if the young person is affected by what has been termed 'incomplete mourning,' has in effect been unable to achieve the catharsis of grief, and so carries within himself through later years an insufferable burden of rage . . . guilt . . . sorrow."

So my daughter Nancy, who tells me I was her nurturing parent, may have been suffering from "incomplete mourning" for the departure, the "abandonment" by her father, and now finds all that pain and grief evoked by the dying and death of her mother. Nancy is a dancer. Like Zorba, her way to work through, embody, and incarnate her grief is by dancing it. Two years ago I saw her perform her master's thesis dance at Smith College. It was a choreography of dark passage with her mother, cradling her, letting her go, coming into a circle of healing song and leaping hope. She integrated dance, music, song, and poetry in her piece, titled *Haloweyo*, a word that symbolizes the choice to continue to commit body and soul to the act of living. Nancy's poem text:

You leant heavily into me as we walked together
    slowly down the road

Your tentative steps, once strong strides
No words are spoken, but hearts entwine
Softly, slowly, no words

You ask a question, soft and simple now like a child
But you see deeper than anyone now
You are further along than I
Slowly and gradually withdrawing from this world,
       from your loved ones, from me

Your hair is so soft now, like a baby's, and gray its
       natural color
Your eyes peer out, trusting but frightened
Woman whose direction and purpose had been so clear
And now the strength is gone
But the wisdom is deeper
Understanding goes deep into the bones now
As your body melts, your spirit rises, going through
       fear
But now I am left to answer the yearnings
My flesh shreds as you pull away

Now I find you curled into your acorn of self
Becoming absorbed again by your soul
Encased in another womb you are waiting and growing

You watch for me in the twilight of my dreams
I feed you with the bread of my life
We know we are a part of each other
We know we are one thing.

   As for Nancy and me, the dance of our healing goes
on gently, gladly, and with love. And we do not dance

alone. Poet Howard Nemerov begins his poem on hearing Pablo Casals' recording of Bach's Sixth Suite:

Deep in a time that cannot come again
Bach thought it through, this lonely and immense
Reflexion wherein our sorrows learn to dance.
And deep in the time that cannot come again
Casals recorded it.

And deep in our own time we may find ourselves dancing with multitudes of friends and strangers, finding our own authentic space in the world, moving beyond private grief into public sorrow, and bearing our own peculiar witness. When we embrace our sorrow, affirming our commitment to life, we struggle to transform catastrophe into tragedy, wrest some meaning from the mystery, and seek in sorrow a blessing.

Questions for pondering:

What is the deepest loss you have suffered in your life?

Is there a certain grief or loss you have been denying?

How has sorrow been a storehouse of nourishment for you?

What has it meant, what might it mean, for you to spread your wings in the valley of your sorrow?

✳

3. *Savoring Blessedness*

My fiftieth year had come and gone,
I sat, a solitary man,
In a crowded London shop,
An open book and empty cup
On the marble table-top.

While on the shop and street I gazed
My body of a sudden blazed;
And twenty minutes more or less
It seemed, so great my happiness,
That I was blessed and could bless.
                                        —W. B. Yeats

N aming and embracing our sorrow frees us to recognize as well the blessedness of our lives. We may count our blessings, taking time to *remember* and gather special moments or occasions of great happiness—especially those experiences of mutual blessing, those occasions of grace when we realize that in a given situation or relationship we are both blessed and blessing.

We may *retrieve* these gifted moments by writing them in a journal or telling them to someone. Either of those acts can facilitate the resurrection of events long buried in deep memory, bringing them into life once again, releasing a fresh surge of their original joy.

At our age there is a new readiness to *savor* such

occasions and to recognize oneself as a blessed and blessing person. It is time to taste the vintage wine of one's life, taking pleasure in its bouquet and flavor.

Yeats's poem (quoted above), in describing the context of his revelation of great happiness, provides images filled with energy for remembering and savoring one's own blessedness. If blessedness is the text of this chapter, the context consists of those special circumstances that make us, like Yeats, ripe and ready to be apprehended by grace. Before focusing on our experiences of mutual blessedness, we are invited to ruminate over these images as suits our particular circumstances.

My fiftieth year had come and gone

The fiftieth birthday is often an occasion for special acknowledgment, a rare if not unique milestone in the life cycle. How did you celebrate this marker event? Yeats, sitting in that shop, was pondering his own fiftieth year. What had happened in his life to bring him to the brink of revelation? What had he been doing that week? Was he meeting someone at that shop, or just stopping off for a spot of tea? Was the shop familiar to him or strange? Why did the passing of his fiftieth year open a trapdoor into blessing?

While we can only speculate about Yeats, it may be possible to get a close-up of our own experience. We can never anticipate or prevent such a moment of transformation. But a birthday, an anniversary, a wedding, a funeral, a holiday, or a reunion may open the floodgates of recollection. We may imagine we are taking this particular event in stride and then, in the kitchen or at a desk, on the street or anywhere, we may be overwhelmed with a boundless gratitude.

I sat, a solitary man

What has made you solitary? What decisions of your own, accidents, or choices of others have carved the contours of your journey, broken the predictable mold of your plans, and taken you, careening, down strange and fearsome paths? My decision for divorce broke up the unity and security of my life, dislodged my relationships with children and parents, put me in professional jeopardy, and shattered my simplistic images of myself as good and duty-bound, and of God as the conventional arbiter of right and wrong. Suddenly, it seemed, paradox, darkness, contradiction were contending in me. I had been living in what I supposed to be the light for all these years, only now to discover an enormous quantity of dark matter in the universe of my own soul.

The death of a relationship, a loved one, or a dream, or the loss of job, health, or freedom tears us out of a secure and predictable context, throwing us onto a path of individuation. One finds oneself groping in the dark, attacked, like the biblical Jacob, by an unknown adversary, fighting for life, refusing to let go until a blessing is received. One thrashes in the struggle of self-differentiation, the travail of becoming a singular, solitary man or woman, though women's individuation often seems to take a different path from that of men.

Anatoly Sharansky became a solitary person when he was arrested by the KGB on a Moscow street in 1977 at the age of twenty-nine. Accused of treason and espionage, he was imprisoned for nine years and was frequently threatened with death. In fact, he had been publicly fighting for the right of Soviet Jews to emigrate to Israel and was an active member of the Helsinki Watch Committee, which monitored Soviet compliance with that accord. In his book *Fear No Evil*, he relates how he resisted the efforts of the KGB to break him and force him to recant. His wife, Avital, smuggled a psalmbook to him soon after his imprisonment. Though raised as a secular Jew and not a practicing believer, he learned Hebrew in order to read the book, and came to know most of the psalms by heart. When taken for interrogation he would repeat one of the psalms to himself to bolster his courage. He found astonishing resonance between his own fearful bondage and the oppression suffered by many of his psalm-writing ancestors. Their prayers became his own, heartening him and helping to preserve his sanity and hope.

At one point the KGB took the psalmbook from him. He refused any cooperation with them until they returned the book. He was thrown into the terrible "punishment cell," where he endured one hundred and eighty-six solitary days and nights. He held out for that book, palpable nourishment for the marrow of his soul, keeping open the "interconnection of souls," which so encouraged him. His health deteriorated seriously, and fearing that he might die in the cell, the KGB returned the psalmbook to him. When he was finally freed, the only personal possession he took with him out of prison was the psalmbook. He then emigrated to Israel, where he changed his first name to

Natan, the biblical prophet who spoke up to King David.

Sharansky came through his solitary ordeal a blessed and blessing man, an encouraging companion for us in our own solitary ordeals. He inspires me to pray: "Lord, give me this day my daily bread of courage. Increase my strength of soul to resist the fears within me, the pressures upon me, and the seductions around me, and keep me from shading my truth or compromising my integrity for any reason, be it another dollar, a pat on the back, a favor, or a privilege. Whether my punishment cell is a sick body, an abiding depression, a broken relationship or trust, a professional hope disappointed, a grief that will not weep itself out, or being stuck in an oppressive system, comfort me in the dark silence, and enable me to stand and withstand in the evil day."

When one suffers one's own solitary ordeal one is on the way to blessedness, the way of solitude.

Poet Denise Levertov writes, "Your solitudes utter their own runes, your own voices begin to rise in your throats." A rune is a whisper, a mystery, a riddle, a secret sign or sound. Your rune reveals the etymology of your soul and is your means of echolocation within your deep self. Deep calls to deep. The prophet Elijah, at the mouth of a cave, heard his own rune in a still, small voice: the whisper of vocation, the sound of his future. What is the rune of your solitude?

My friend shifts uneasily in his chair; he is uncomfortable; his chest aches. He is pregnant with himself. Something is happening. *He* is happening. Stories frozen for decades in his soul begin to melt and pour out. It has been so long since he has heard his own voice. His eyes stop glancing by my head and look into my eyes. The truth of his inward being calls forth the truth of mine. Rune calls to rune.

People, houses, lakes, mountains, rocks, rivers, trees, and animals have runes. Our collie, Joshua, groans softly as he dreams; it sounds like a whale song, the sonar of his soul. I stroke his back and am comforted. I am looking and listening for runes these days. When I see the color purple, I smile at Alice Walker. When I hear "Georgia on My Mind," I croon with Ray Charles. Runes invite us to be hidden colleagues, spiritual friends. Runes ride on waves through centuries, across continents, heedless of death. Rune calls to rune.

We are ready now, at our age, for our solitude to utter its own rune. We are ready now to acknowledge the ache in our chest, to hear our own voice rising in the throat, the sound of our future. The solitary wait on the edge of blessedness.

In a crowded London shop

What is the crowd scene of your life? Does it include frenetic work involvements, a complicated family life, a variety of social commitments and causes? If you are retired, is your life still crowded with activity? A retired friend said to me proudly and perhaps gratefully, "I've never been busier in my life!" We certainly want to have things to do when we're no longer working full-time, but many of us also want some leisure to *be*, and yearn for those years to be about more than keeping busy.

My psyche is a crowd: I am a multitude, my name

is legion. I'm not talking about multiple personality disorder here but about the many voices and faces of my soul. Once I was on a subway train, looking out the window at people milling around. The train pulled out of the station, lurched into a tunnel, and suddenly I stared into my own startled face reflected in the window. I am glad to be old enough to see my face in focus. It is much wrinkled, like my mother's. But it is my face. I have earned and I deserve it, for better and for worse.

When in New York City, I often leave the crowd and go to the Frick Museum. It is a small museum, manageable in an hour or so. But I always wind up on the second floor, sitting on a bench looking, for some minutes, at one of Rembrandt's self-portraits. The bulbous nose, the solid head, the sadness in the eyes, the unflinching self-knowledge, the mundane humility of this man. I usually notice something new, something that had escaped me before, because I have changed a little since last we looked at each other. It comforts and awakens me to sit with him. The truth of his inward being calls forth the truth of my own. Rune calls to rune. My soul is quiet. I wonder if I too am being seen and known.

An open book . . .

What was Yeats's book? Where was it open? Had he come upon a passage that caused him to ponder awhile? What might your book be in such a place? These days I am reading biographies, novels, poetry, and often the Bible. I was rummaging around in Psalm 119 one morning, delighting in the trove of nourishing phrases: "Let your steadfast love become my comfort . . . turn to me and be gracious to me as is your custom towards those who love your name . . . I treasure your word in my heart." I spoke those last words aloud, tasted them, savored them. Memories flooded in of scripture and hymn verses learned by heart as a child in a minister's household. In his book *Patrimony*, Philip Roth writes that his father gave him the vernacular, the street language of Newark in the 1930s. My father gave me the Bible, the faith language of Minneapolis in the 1930s. The liturgy crept into my bones.

Our old folk, following the author of the Ninetieth Psalm, teach us "to number our days that we may get a heart of wisdom." Bessie Addams was ninety-four when she died. As one of her pastors, I visited her at home in her later years and learned how she coped when she woke at night and couldn't get back to sleep. She would start repeating verses of scripture beginning with the letter *A*, then *B*, and so on through the alphabet until she fell asleep. In her own way she took the words of Psalm 119 to heart: "I remember your name in the night, O Lord." Words that comfort, disturb, intrigue, heal, illumine us become our open book, holy in our hearts.

We cannot yet read our life, because it is still reading us. The book remains open. As we review it by rereading journals, revisiting familiar places and people, leafing through photo albums, watching old home movies, we may notice some things we missed in the living of those years. There is my father turning the crank on the ice cream maker, holding out the paddle to the lucky kid who got to lick off the delicious ice cream, Dad running into the lake, laughing,

Dad on the big tire in the lake, we children tipping him over. There is Mother in the background, not wanting her picture taken, a curious detachment in her face. Why? What did she know? What sadness did she harbor?

One day the summer after my father died, I was rummaging around in the garage at the family cottage in Michigan. I came upon four bundles with the names Rose, Richard, John, and Robert on them. Opening the one with my name, I found scores of letters I had written my parents all through my life, the earliest at seven years of age from summer camp, a carefully tear-stained plea for them to come and get their homesick child. They didn't. There were also copies of many letters my father had written to me. I sat down and began revisiting my life through the correspondence, which he, sixty years ago, began saving, for my siblings and me to discover after his death. It was like finding buried treasure.

My father was the most powerful, shaping person in my life. I adored him, as he had adored his father, for whom I was named. My divorce angered and saddened him. I felt judged by him, and he felt betrayed by me. Though our broken relationship healed, to a large degree, before his death, I think he was never able to understand how I could do what I had to do.

We are stuck with our fathers and mothers, and they with us. Some men long to hear their father say "I love you," and it never happens. Men gather in a meeting room at Kirkridge. In an exercise by psychologist and author Sam Osherson, they are asked to write down on a card the most shameful or humiliating experience they ever had with their father. The cards are gathered, shuffled, and then redistributed. In the quiet, one by one, the cards are read aloud, and the room is filled with the anguish and anger of father-wounded men. Later in the workshop men are invited to remember a gift given to them by their father and, still later, a gift they would like to give their father. The intent of the workshop is to provide a context in which men may begin to heal the wounded father within their psyche. Men seek their fathers, and women, their mothers, dead or alive, down the years. Dylan Thomas wrote, "And you, my father, there on the sad height / Curse, bless me now with your fierce tears, I pray." We have been both cursed and blessed by our parents, and our children by us.

The book of our life remains open, even beyond the death of loved ones. While much at our age would seem to be closed—roads not taken, doors slammed shut—we still have the opportunity of finding treasure hidden in the pages of our years. It is never too late for a little more healing in recollection.

An open book and empty cup

What had Yeats been drinking? Coffee, tea? What might be in your cup? While it is nice to have a full cup or even one "running over," there is one great virtue in an empty cup—room for thirst, for craving. An empty cup leaves choices open: what to put in the cup, whether to fill it up halfway, whether to take a sip or bolt it down in one swallow. The writer of the Forty-second Psalm cries, "As a hart longs for flowing streams, so longs my soul for thee, O God. My soul thirsts for God . . . for the living God." Is it still pos-

sible for the water of my years to be turned into wine?
If so, make it a dark Italian red, perhaps Chianti. Is
transformation still available to me? How can one be
born anew when one is old?

There is in us a deep yearning for the later years to
be significant, filled with personal growth, intellectual
stimulation, and continuing contribution to family
and society. Perhaps that's why it is my tendency to
fill my cup quickly, more or less with anything, so that
I will not feel the pain of emptiness or the fear of non-
being. I am impatient of satisfaction, though in these
later years I am able to tolerate a little waiting, letting
choices mature, allowing things to unfold, less often
rushing to decision, and even, sometimes, refusing to
decide now. An empty cup is filled with choices not
yet made, hours, days unlived.

Maybe now is a good time to let the cup stay
empty awhile, suffer the pangs of uncertainty and lack
of closure. Maybe now is a time to refuse, resist, fast,
pare down, edit our life, shed no-longer-needed
things and obsolete attitudes, activate the nos in order
to clear the way for yeses waiting in the wings. It's
okay to resign from this committee or that obligation.
We have been on plenty of committees and fulfilled
lots of duties. We don't need to justify or explain ourselves anymore. We are old enough to choose how
we want to spend our time and serve our community
without fear of social disapproval or economic
reprisal. It is time to pay attention to our thirst and
seek what could water our dry soul. Quality matters
now, not quantity. If we have gulped down experiences and years, it is time now to learn how to savor
each day's gift, to look and really see, to listen and

really hear. We can allow ourselves to be more sen-
suous, more earthy, more present to pleasure as well as
pain. Golf and travel, pleasurable as they may be,
won't satisfy our deepest longings. A woman wrote
me, "I've found that I can be lonely in most of the
capitals of the world." What *will* satisfy? Might our
cup be filled somehow, someday, with blessing?

On the marble table-top.

Marble is cold, with the coldness of pillars, tomb-
stones, institutional walls. The book and cup seem to
sit on death, my death. I hear my daughter and her
husband planning retirement in twenty-five years—
when I will surely be dead. The thought of my death
is acceptable, in the distance, but I feel its cold breath
now in their plans for a world without me. I am getting more comfortable with, if not quite comforted
by, thoughts of my death.

Yet marble also connotes endurance, stability, the
venerability of age, stone carved and crafted. Marble is
something to be counted on. It has been there for
aeons and will be there long after we're gone. It
bespeaks continuity and durability. It is the ancient
rock of the mountains, those hills to which we lift up
our eyes and from where our help comes. Nothing
startles the rock of ages. We can bring anything to
this mountaintop or tabletop: our egregious sins,
secret delights, and outrageous fantasies. This is an
abiding table where we are welcome and where all are
welcome.

Consider the memorable tables of your life:
kitchen table, dining table, bedside, boardroom, and
communion table. Shapes and purposes vary, but these

are the tables around which family, friends, colleagues, adversaries have sat with you. Remember the tables of first, last, and many suppers. Imagine the great oak table on which the Camp David peace accord between Israel and Egypt was signed in 1978, the same table on which the Israel-Palestinian peace agreement was signed in 1993. So much tension and fear, so much fierce hope around so many tables. Some tables have been turned, others kicked over. Now is the time to bring the gifts of your life to the table: to remember, retrieve, and savor your special occasions of blessedness.

While on the shop and street I gazed
My body of a sudden blazed;
And twenty minutes more or less
It seemed, so great my happiness,
That I was blessed and could bless.

Yeats experienced a moment of blessedness that he would savor the rest of his life. He did not initiate it, though he was ripe and accessible to it. Such moments or events are treasures. The most transformative involve hearts and bodies strangely warmed, and often partake of mutual blessedness. The experience may consist of an inner realization or take the form of outer embodiment. One may be gazing out on a London street or walking in Philadelphia when the strange epiphany occurs.

A friend in her sixties wrote me about such an occasion:

It happened during the Christmas season. I was walking down Chestnut Street when I noticed a large group of people concentrating on some object. As I approached, I saw a little girl about seven years old who was obviously lost, sobbing and bewildered. She was pulling away from all those who tried to take her hand and comfort her, including the young policeman who was endeavoring to interest her in his horse. Something impelled me to walk through that crowd of people, and when I reached the inner circle, I stooped down and reached out my arms without saying a word. Almost instantly the little girl turned around and our eyes met. Then she put out her arms—straight out, just as I held mine—and came toward me. She was a large child, and ordinarily I would not attempt to lift one so heavy, but as she came confidently and unhesitatingly into my arms, I enfolded her and stood up. She entwined her arms and legs around my body and struggled to get closer and closer until we were almost a single figure. We stood in that position for a long time without uttering a single word. I did not ask her name, nor did she say anything at all to me, but she was quiet, relaxed, and contented. The small crowd around us did not move or converse. There was complete silence.

It must have been fully ten minutes that we clung together before something made me turn and I saw a young woman with blue eyes—I remember so poignantly those calm eyes—standing close by. She had evidently just approached us. It was then I uttered the first words I had spoken since discovering the little one. "Does she belong to you?"

"Yes," the woman replied, and then the child disengaged herself from my arms, quietly slid down to the sidewalk, and silently the two walked off together. The mother did not thank me nor did the child give me a glance. They disappeared in the holiday throng as though nothing at all had happened. I turned and began walking away and felt a peculiar exaltation and buoyancy I had never experienced before. My chest almost ached with the wonder that swelled within me, for I knew I had been a vehicle for a divine purpose—and that miracles do happen!

Miracle on Chestnut Street. Ten minutes more or less. One can only marvel at such an encounter and savor its joy. Has there been an occasion in your life when a conversation with a stranger on a plane, or eye contact across a crowded room, or an unintended touch at a party or meeting connected you and another in a moment of mutual recognition that might have changed your life, or did? The gift of *stranger-blessedness* may invite you across conventional boundaries. Sometimes, when you welcome a stranger, you find that you are entertaining an angel unawares.

Poet Pablo Neruda was raised in Temuco, a frontier town in southern Chile. He remembers the main street as lined with hardware stores, which, since the local population couldn't read, hung out eye-catching signs: "an enormous saw, a giant cooking pot . . . a mammoth spoon . . . a colossal boot." Playing in the lot behind his house one day when he was still a little boy, Neruda discovered a hole in a fence board:

> I looked through the hole and saw landscape uncared for, and wild. I moved back a few steps, because I sensed vaguely that something was about to happen. All of a sudden a hand appeared—a tiny hand of a boy about my own age. By the time I came close again, the hand was gone, and in its place there was a marvelous white toy sheep. The sheep's wool was faded. . . . Its wheels had escaped . . . [yet] I had never seen such a wonderful sheep. I looked back through the hole but the boy had disappeared. I went into the house and brought out a treasure of my own: a pine cone, opened, full of odor and resin, which I adored. I set it down in the same spot and went off with the sheep. I never saw either the hand or the boy again. . . . This exchange of gifts—mysterious— settled deep inside me like a sedimentary deposit. . . . I have been a lucky man. To feel the intimacy of brothers is a marvelous thing in life. . . . But to feel the affection that comes from those whom we do not know . . . who are watching over our sleep and solitude, over our dangers and our weaknesses—that is something still greater and more beautiful because it widens out the boundaries of our being, and unites all living things.
>
> That exchange brought home to me for the first time a precious idea: that all humanity is somehow together. . . . It won't surprise you then

that I have attempted to give something resiny, earthlike and fragrant in exchange for human brotherhood.

And thus Neruda credits his childhood moment of wondrous revelation with the impetus to become a writer. Do you have occasions of childhood happiness waiting in your deep memory for retrieval and savoring? I remember my childhood scantily. But I do have one memory of an incident, which, though not conventionally laudable, seeded me with a confidence of being loved whether I deserved it or not. It was summer, and our family was vacationing in a cottage on a lake in northern Minnesota. I was four or five years old. One day I got into a fight with another boy on a dock. Suddenly, I heard my mother's voice. She had come around a building about a hundred feet from the dock, saw me and the other boy fighting, and, with no clue as to who was responsible, hollered: "Give it to him, Bob!" Thus encouraged, I proceeded to do just that. I recognized in that moment my mother's glorious prejudice on my behalf, and knew that she would always be in my corner, no matter what. I might do wrong, and did, or embarrass her and my father, and did, but from that moment on, I never doubted that she would be there for me. Her maternal loyalty funded a self-confidence that has strengthened me through good times and bad to this day, as I savor the memory of that *childhood blessedness*.

While my father and I communicated over the years by writing letters, my son Bob and I talk on the phone frequently and at great length. Different eras, different modes of communicating. I marvel now at the special moments that we have shared on the phone: the call when he told me he had gotten into the college of his choice; the call, after midnight, when he told me he had gotten into a marvelous singing group at college; the call about getting into medical school. And then a call bearing unexpected bad news. Bob had applied to several hospital programs for an orthopedic residency and, in the matching system used by medical students and programs, had not been accepted by any. He had done well academically in medical school, so it was a great shock when he wasn't accepted. It was a serious, and perhaps fatal, setback to his hopes of getting into an orthopedic program. But he took it well, and arranged to get into a general surgery program for one year in Chicago, where his wife, also a medical student, had been accepted in an OB-GYN residency. In the months that followed, though the odds weren't good, he pursued every possible lead to find another orthopedic program for which he might apply. One night he called to tell me he was one of five applicants for an opening at the University of Chicago, and a few weeks later came the call when he told me, "Dad, they've offered me a place!"

He was overjoyed. I was overjoyed, so happy for him, and for myself. It was as though all the years of our being father and son had now borne fruit in his finding a way to pursue his vocation. I smile whenever I remember that call, and rejoice again in all that his achievement meant for him. Disappointments of many kinds will come, but nobody can take away that moment of joy. I am eternally grateful, and savor again and again that twenty minutes, more or less, in which

I felt so great a happiness in being, in this way, a blessed and blessing father.

One opens up the album of family memories carefully, and with some trepidation. As in every family, one shares a common and burdened history. Birthdays and holidays may carry memories of anger and hurt from the past. You may have vowed never to try *that* holiday again with the whole family. Tensions between parents and children, between stepparents and stepchildren, between siblings, between spouses, and among any other combination of family members are often there underground, biding their time, like a minefield from a war of long ago. There are so many ways special family celebrations can be sabotaged deliberately or inadvertently.

But now and then good things happen. One year Cindy and I discussed inviting all six of our children and their partners and children to spend Thanksgiving with us. Though it was a daunting prospect, we decided to give it a shot, figuring that only three or four of them would be able to make it. We sent an invitation in the form of the sort of flyer Kirkridge sends out for an event. It was titled *A Country Thanksgiving*, described as a unique gathering of the Hirni-Raines extended, blended families, including "a rich range of activities for your holiday pleasure: a traditional Thanksgiving feast, walks in the woods, swimming at the Y, football viewing, Katie watching, playtime with [our dog] Joshua, hearts and other games of mischance, singing, dancing, baby tending, endless conversations, the joy of the company of Hirni and Raines, and other delights too numerous to mention. A highlight of the gathering will be the baptism of the newborn baby of Nancy and Juan Carlos." The cost was identified as "nothing but your undying gratitude." It turned out to be a foolhardy offer: they *all* came, with their significant others, granddaughter Katie, and newly born Kyle.

On Thanksgiving night, we gathered in front of the fireplace in the living room for Kyle's baptism. I took him in my arms, and looked at his mother and father and the family gathered. As I placed my hand on his warm head, it seemed to me that all our family struggles, successes, sorrows, hopes had come to focus in this moment. Touching Kyle seemed to me to connect all of us in that room, and the generations before and after, in an eternal communion. Joy flooded my heart. Suddenly, Kyle cried out as babies will do, there was laughter, the precious moment was gone, and the time of the ritual was at hand. Twenty seconds "more or less / It seemed, so great my happiness, / That I was blessed and could bless."

But as it turned out, it was much longer than that. Our friend Jim came and took a photograph of all us gathered. Years later, it remains the only photo of all the members of our family together. The photo is in our bedroom. Now and then its faces catch me up, and I savor again the blessedness of that occasion. There will come separation, departure, death. In family photos of the future, some who are in this picture may be absent, and others may be present. But there our family is, happy together on that blessed Thanksgiving Day. Nothing and nobody can take that away. Such an occasion, like a family heirloom, is to be treasured and savored in memory and hope.

In addition to occasions of *family-blessedness*, we

may have experienced a solitary blessedness that delights and fulfills us. Betty Friedan tells such a story: "I met Jeannie Roth in Apsen. . . . She was sixty-five. She had been a housewife and a volunteer until her husband left her for his young secretary. At sixty-one, she went to work for the first time, as a . . . telephone operator for a ski company. She had come to Colorado to an Elderhostel in Durango and just stayed on . . . [Before long] Elderhostels had become a way of life for her. She had just come back from three weeks in Turkey, learned to speak French in Montreal, studied whooping cranes in their natural habitat on the Gulf of Mexico, and gone on an archeological dig in Kenya. She told me, . . . 'I love my single life, I call it "single-blessedness." I love to travel, visit my children and friends as a single person.' "

What a woman! What a human being! There she goes re-inventing her life out of seeming disaster, and by wit and imagination discovering the joys of *single-blessedness*. If I ever have to learn that art and vocation, Jeannie Roth will be one of my mentors. Another will be Claire Strandberg, a housewife, mother, and volunteer for decades until her husband, Ken, died. Then in her fifties, she went to seminary, became a minister, engaged in interim ministries, and eventually wound up as pastor of a congregation in New Zealand for two years, when cancer took her life. She wrote me shortly after her husband's death. "I miss Ken. I can never have him back. When I talk with people I entreat them to care for their own life, individually first and together second. When your work comes first, and it fails, where is your life? If your spouse comes first, and they leave or die, where is your life? If children are your life, and they move out as they must into their own lives, where is your life? My life is larger than each of these primary relationships, and I must learn to care for my life, nurture, nourish, relish, love it dearly, for under God no one else can live it for me."

We may, like Claire, miss a former partner or, like Jeannie, find a whole new unencumbered life out there. We may find, as they did, that we can bless ourselves and be blessed in a lifestyle of single-blessedness.

But, if one has a partner, it also makes sense to savor one's *partner-blessedness*. One summer day Cindy and I took what we call a wildflower run along Cherry Valley Road near Kirkridge. We have driven slowly along that road countless times across the years, enjoying the beauty of the rolling farmland and occasionally looking for flowers. That day we spotted purple loosestrife and ironweed, yellow cone flowers, black-eyed Susans, joe-pye weed, and some lavender thistle. Stopping by the side of the road, we picked them, put them in a water bucket in the backseat, stopped farther on, picked a few more, and, mostly in silence, returned home. Cindy arranged the flowers in a large vase for the dining room table and made two smaller bouquets for the living room and our bedroom.

I enjoyed the flowers at dinner that night, and the next morning, noticing their beauty, felt my happiness rekindled. It came to me how much I cherish those times of gathering flowers together. While it is Cindy's gift to arrange them, it is my pleasure to watch her. I enjoy those wildflowers just a bit more than the flowers we buy or pick from the garden. But more, I love being together that way. Much of what we are as partners is alive and present in those moments, which I have come to savor as blessed and blessing occasions. As so often is the case, Blake puts it best: "To see the world in a grain of sand, / And a heaven in a wild flower; / Hold infinity in the palm of your hand, / And eternity in an hour."

I delight in a *daily blessedness* that visits me each morning in the wild birds at our feeders. Since 1978 we have had a bird log, registering our residents, and visitors like rose-breasted grosbeaks, scarlet tanagers, indigo buntings, and other outrageous birds who arrive annually during the first two weeks of May. Yes, I'm bragging, really celebrating the gorgeous invasion of the merry, merry month of May. We put out the seed; they come and get it. It's like O'Hare Airport, arrivals and departures. It's a mutual exchange, a mutual feeding, a mutual blessing. We do not tire of watching cardinals arriving at dawn and dusk, or hearing the distant tom-tom sound the pileated woodpecker makes as it rat-a-tats a dead tree in the forest.

Daily blessedness comes with the territory of the elder passage as we realize, at last, that all we want is more of the same delight: of daily breathing, hearing, seeing, smelling, touching, tasting. It is *life* we want, and we don't want to waste any more of it. So we begin to savor the blessedness of the ordinary.

In our bouquet of blessings, there is probably one named *friendship-blessedness*. This would be our memories of the courage or kindness or sheer love received from a friend. What friends—colleagues, classmates, neighbors, buddies, soul mates—have been there for you in good times and bad? Whose names occur to you? Oscar Wilde, the British writer, came into bankruptcy and was thrown into debtors' prison. He wrote about an unnamed friend:

> When I was brought down from my prison to the Court of Bankruptcy, between two policemen, [my friend] waited in the long dreary corridor that, before the whole crowd, whom an action so sweet and simple hushed into silence, he might gravely raise his hat to me, as, handcuffed and with bowed head, I passed by him. Men have gone to heaven for smaller things than that. It was in this spirit, and with this mode of love, that the saints knelt down to wash the feet of the poor, or stopped to kiss the leper on the cheek. I have never said one single word to him about what he did. I do not know to the present moment whether he is aware that I was even conscious of his action. It is not a thing for which one can render formal thanks in formal words. I store it in the treasure-house of my heart. I keep it there as a secret debt that I am glad to think I can never possibly repay. . . . When wisdom has been profitless to me, philosophy barren, and the proverbs and phrases of those who have sought to give me consolation as dust and ashes in my mouth, the memory of that little, lovely, silent act of love has unsealed for me all the wells of pity, . . . and brought me out of the bitterness of lonely exile into harmony with the wounded, broken, and great heart of the world.

Is there a memory of a friend's little, lovely, silent act of love towards you stored in your heart? A memory with power to comfort and nourish you again and again? A memory whose blessedness you savor with evergreen gratitude? When we suffer some kind of public disgrace at work, in the family, or in the community, a raised-hat gesture of abiding respect in front of everybody is an act of amazing grace that opens the heart of our own compassion for others suffering the bitterness of lonely exile. However private our deepest moments of blessedness, they take us into the great heart of the world, where they add to the beauty of creation and bring us into the *blessed community*, the communion of the saints.

On Christmas Day in 1989 the Brandenburg Gate in the Berlin Wall was opened, and for the first time in twenty-eight years, East and West Berliners were able to mingle freely and pass back and forth. Leonard Bernstein had been invited to conduct an international orchestra in the Schauspielhaus concert hall in East Berlin in celebration of the occasion. It was televised live on PBS, and I decided to watch for a few minutes. I saw people embracing strangers, running into the arms of loved ones and friends not seen or touched in twenty-eight years, laughing, weeping, dancing. My heart was dancing too.

The orchestra was composed of musicians from East and West Germany and from the four occupying powers at the end of World War II—Great Britain, France, the Soviet Union, and the United States. Bernstein chose to conduct Beethoven's Ninth Symphony as the culmination of a three-day festival celebrating the demise of the Wall. He said prior to the performance, "I am experiencing an historical moment incomparable with others in my long, long life." Beethoven's Ninth was inspired by Schiller's eighteenth-century poem "Ode to Joy," from which the hymn "Joyful, Joyful, We Adore Thee" derives. For this concert Bernstein substituted the word "freedom" for the word "joyful" in the chorus, "by the authority of the moment," as he put it. He waved the baton with all the passionate yearning of his seventy-one years, his face pleated with praise; the members of the orchestra and choir were rapt in this liturgy of reconciliation; the audience inside and outside the concert hall was thunderous in applause and, at the end, gave a standing ovation.

As I watched Bernstein, a Jew, conducting a German symphony in the land of the Reformation and the Holocaust, my heart turned over. He was presented by the East German government with the Star of the People's Friendship. Fifty years ago he might instead have worn a yellow star on his shirt and perhaps a pink triangle as well. And instead of the Schauspielhaus he might have been in Auschwitz. Beholding his moment of extraordinary happiness, I burst out singing "Freedom, Freedom, We Adore Thee," my body alive with the joy of participating in spiritual intimacy not only with the concert congregation led by Rabbi Bernstein, but also with those millions who suffered, struggled, prayed, of whom many have died, through all the decades towards this hour. I knew I was in that number, this time, when the saints went marching in and out.

Now, years later, with Bernstein dead, Nazi elements arising once again in Germany and elsewhere in

Europe, and militia paranoia in our own country, one realizes that, in nations as in families, blessed moments guarantee nothing about the future. But such moments live in our hearts to be savored again and again with unalloyed joy, and always with power to enliven hope in the rebirth of human community and to renew commitment to do our part in the great work of healing creation.

One of the psalms I was required to learn by heart as a child was Psalm 103. Its author encourages us to savor blessedness by resting our lives in the blessing of God:

> Bless the Lord, O my soul,
>   and all that is within me, bless [God's] holy name!
> Bless the Lord, O my soul,
>   and forget not all [God's] benefits,
> who forgives all your iniquity,
>   who heals all your diseases,
> who redeems your life from the Pit,
>   who crowns you with steadfast love and mercy,
> who satisfies you with good as long as you live
>   so that your youth is renewed like the eagle's.

In age, our youth renewed with fresh soul energy soars like an eagle, crowned with steadfast love and savoring blessedness.

The deepest part of us wants to give some-thing back, to make a difference, to leave the camp-ground a little better than we found it. We want to make the best use of our knowledge and experience to benefit the community and fulfill our own purpose in life. So it is appropriate now to re-imagine fresh ways in which our work might flourish in the years ahead.

Questions for pondering:

When did you know yourself to be a blessed and blessing person?

What phone call, letter, photo, or conversation is a reservoir of joy?

What are the ingredients of your daily blessedness?

How do you experience being blessed by God?

4· Re-imagining Work

Whatever is foreseen in joy
Must be lived out from day to day,
Vision held open in the dark
By our ten thousand days of work.
Harvest will fill the barn; for that
The hand must ache, the face must sweat.

And yet no leaf or grain is filled
By work of ours; the field is tilled
And left to grace. That we may reap
Great work is done while we're asleep.

When we work well, a Sabbath mood
Rests on our day, and finds it good.
—Wendell Berry

Work and love, as Freud suggested, are the two basic experiences central to our humanity. While in the next chapter we will consider love, the task now is to explore our work, which not only takes most of our waking hours and energy, but also is a major vehicle for our creativity and a container of our identity. We begin by reviewing our work history in order to apprehend in memory and reflection what work roles, chosen or imposed, have defined us to others and ourselves in early and middle adulthood. Whether your work has been primarily in the marketplace or in the home, recognizing and naming your past and current work roles constitute a first step towards *re-imagining* work in the elder passage and on into the elder season. Some may have the option to keep on working at the same job, or in the same field, for many more years. Some may choose or be forced to retire from full-time employment. David Dodson Gray writes, "Most women know that at least one of their jobs, their 'other career of homemaker,' will go on until they drop or enter a nursing home. Husbands retire but wives never do." Some may have to earn money to supplement pension and Social Security; others already have financial security. Some, worn down and worn out by their commitments and exertions, may anticipate being relieved of the burdens of work, and look forward to travel, more time for family and friends, and the delight of leisure. Others may fear retirement, and wonder if there is life after work.

Most of us want to find ways to keep on contributing, to give back, to stay involved, to make a difference, to have the courage to do new things and to take risks. But how might we do these things? How might we connect our hard-earned wisdom and compassion with the myriad needs of society to yield another harvest in the elder season? We sense that there may be creativity in ourselves and in our social context that could be teased out, if we allow our imagination to wander, meander, play around a bit.

Could we find a root metaphor capacious enough to carry the meaning of work throughout a lifetime, an image that would help us evaluate our past work with honest appreciation and imagine our future work with excitement and joy? The poem introducing this chapter is evocative for me.

Whatever is foreseen in joy
Must be lived out from day to day,
Vision held open in the dark
By our ten thousand days of work.

It came my way when my daughter Nancy was seven and a half months pregnant with her first child. She had been telling me of her daily exercises, the training of the midwives, the lumbering about the house. She spoke of intermittent fears about her first birthing, and of trusting in the "trinity" of the baby's initiative, the wisdom of her own body, and the presence or action of God in the process of her birthing. She was engaging in daily labor towards the Great Labor. I thought the poem spoke of her work, and recited it to her over the phone.

She reminded me that ten thousand is an archetypal number and that the Chinese speak of the "ten thousand things"—all the things that are necessary to the occasion, essential for fulfilling a particular task or making up a life. I remembered "the valley of ten thousand smokes" in North Carolina, Minnesota as "the land of ten thousand lakes," and the verse in "Amazing Grace": "When we've been there ten thousand years, / Bright shining as the sun, / We've no less days to sing God's praise [*or* do our work] / Than when we first begun." Whether the harvest of our work is produce, product, machine, knowledge, art, a well-raised child, or a newborn baby, it must be lived out day by day, in ordinary ways and places. We must do our own part of the work and allow another part of the work to be done in and through us. The work itself has its own timing, process, and mystery.

Nancy's baby, my grandson Kyle, whom we had "foreseen in joy," was born in good time. And since then I've been imagining the work of our lives as a matter of *holding vision open in the dark*: doing what only we can do—our ten thousand days of work—towards something new being born into the world. Whatever our occupation, job, profession, or vocation has been or now is, we may consider ourselves persons who have held vision open in the dark, doing something useful, even valuable, by our work in the world. All of us may regard ourselves, in this sense, as midwives, assisting at the birthings of people, institutions, products, relationships, even and especially ourselves.

Notwithstanding gender stereotypes, men as well as women may participate in the work of holding vision open in the dark. Men have an unexpected mentor in the Holy Family. A few years ago my wife and I were in the French coastal town of Aigues-Mortes. While walking through the eleventh-century cathedral there, we wandered into a side chapel. There in the center was the traditional Madonna and Child in sculpted stone. But that was not all: off to the side there was a slim wooden sculpture of a man holding a baby. I looked more closely. The man was cradling the baby in his arms, his head bent down in the tender gesture of touching the baby's head with his chin. Underneath the man and child were the identifying words: "Saint Joseph." How beautiful! I had never seen an image of Joseph holding the baby Jesus. In the traditional crèche scene, Joseph was always off in the shadows holding a lantern for everyone else to see *Mary* holding Jesus. The sculpture is to me a blessed reminder that men as well as women are able and called to nurture new life, that nurturing is a *human* vocation.

An ancient biblical text reminds us that without vision the people perish. As a nation and as individuals, we need new visions and dreams, rooted in our core values and derived from our various faiths' traditions, to energize us in creating, together, a peaceful and just commonwealth. Every person, by his or her own work, providing it is honest, useful, and not harmful, makes an indispensable contribution to this Great Work of the universe. One of the joys of age is to be able to see more clearly how one's efforts sustain and are sustained by the work of others, and indeed all living things, in the mysterious work of the Source of all being.

Reviewing Work Life

To recollect the work seasons of our early and middle adulthood, it is helpful to prepare a brief work autobiography. I will be reflecting on my own work history as a white, well-educated male professional, with the limitations and particularities of that experience. As your life and work experience have followed different or even reverse patterns to my own, you will want to make your own appropriate translations and corrections. As you view the "slides" I present to identify my work in early and middle adulthold, my hope is that your slides of these seasons of your work history will pop into focus; and while I come up with two slides, you may identify more. The purpose of the process is to discern the developmental and differentiating character of our work life more clearly. We gather meaning, and allow ourselves to imagine future meaning, by recognizing and naming ourselves in our different seasons of work. Part of who we are is who we were.

When I was a parish minister in early adulthood, the juices flowed. I dreamed dreams, served three different congregations, wrote books, throwing myself passionately into my work, experiencing what British psychologist Elliott Jacques calls "hot from the fire creativity." I was ambitious, consumed with being successful in my field. I was out night after night gathering people together in small Bible-study groups, where they (and I) could tell stories, and working with others in the community on matters of justice and reconciliation. I was a minister from the moment I hopped out of bed in the morning till I sank back into it at night. While I struggled to be a good husband, father, son, and friend, most of my energy and passion poured into my work.

I loved my work. In his book *Care of the Soul*, Thomas Moore writes: "But we are also loved by our work. It can excite us, comfort us, and make us feel fulfilled, just as a lover can. Soul and the erotic are always together. If our work doesn't have an erotic tone to it, then it probably lacks soul as well." If our work was *very* soulful, it is possible there wasn't much erotic energy left for relationships or connection with the earth. If we were "married to our work," climbing up the long ladder of whatever success we were seeking, we may have been failing in other areas of our life. As for me, I worked hard, enjoyed the excitement and productivity of those years, and cherished the friends made, projects completed, causes furthered, and recognition granted, while suffering disappointments, defeats, and, hidden from my consciousness, deep soul-wounds.

As I look back now I can see that during those years my soul virtually disappeared into my role. My work defined my life. Who was I? I was Robert the Minister.

In your early adulthood, what was the major work role, whether in the marketplace or the home, that defined the meaning of your life? Where did your erotic energy go? Were you able to maintain healthy distance between your soul and your role, or were you, like me, occupied, taken over by your work? I have the sense that those women whose primary role in early adulthood was housewife-mother were likewise vulnerable to being taken over, swamped, defined by their role. Whereas it seems to me that women who also worked outside the home were more often able to *have* roles than disappear into them, though also more vulnerable to being stretched beyond their limits. How would you name yourself?

Sometime during our midlife passage, from early into middle adulthood, something may crack the shell of our souls, popping us out of our work-role fixation into a new focus. Some of us get quite a pop; others may not notice any dislocation of life structure while negotiating the midlife passage. Some come staggering out of their tomb like Lazarus, causing a great stink; others stay inside a while longer, rotting.

My ambition moved off center stage when the

suffocation of a dissatisfying marriage, and the inner burgeoning of cloistered vitalities repressed by the pastoral role, were catalyzed by a new and compelling love. These converging energies erupted, breaking me out of my enthrallment in work and casting me into a fearful struggle for my own humanity. (I have written of this midlife passage in my book *Going Home*.) These yearnings, which would not be quelled, and the resulting outer dislocations in marriage and job broke my work addiction. If it was not clear who I would be in the frightening but exhilarating time ahead, it was already clear that I was no longer just Robert the Minister. Anger, grief, and sexual energy poured out of me. Robert was loose in the world and would never again be the prisoner of any work role. As Moore writes, "It is in the nature of things to be drawn to the very experiences that will spoil our innocence, transform our lives, and give us necessary complexity and depth." Robert became less nice and more real.

A lot more of me was now available for living, but my work structure as it had been was gone and a new one not even imagined, much less built. In the meantime, I looked for guidance and comfort where I could find it. I read about a young man who wrote psychiatrist Carl Jung, telling him of his promotion at work. Jung wrote back, offering the young man his condolences, saying that he would stop growing now, because soul treasure is hidden, not in success, but in loss, grief, sorrow, failure. I began looking for such treasure. It was for me a time of "coming out" from a professionally defined self into a personal self, the private and public selves struggling to come into a healthier balance or congruence. For the first time in my adult life I had a chance to grope my way towards integrity of being and doing.

For all of us, such awakenings can yield fresh insight into our work life and lead to a decision to stay where we are or to make changes of role or field, or most important, allow us to discern what matters most in our lives, and how our work might fit more appropriately into the whole picture. If there was no coming out or awakening in your midlife passage, if you breezed through it at full speed, with no detours, you may have entered into a long stagnation, inner baggage piling up to require painful attention later in the elder passage.

I was forty-eight years old when I died to career, if not quite to some form of ministry. I landed at Kirkridge Retreat and Study Center in 1974, grateful for any job, and for this one in particular. I would work there, it turned out, for twenty years, investing the prime time of middle age, and, in recent years, beginning to negotiate the elder passage. Kirkridge was the place where I sought to hold vision open in the dark of people's lives and society's pain. The role of a retreat director holds little power and is comfortable for both director and retreatants. Expectations are limited, projections modest, and mutual responsibilities clear. The role felt like an old and very comfortable corduroy jacket that I could put on and take off, leaving me the same person either way. It was a tremendous privilege to participate in the lives of extraordinary people over those twenty years and to have a modest role in working for peace and justice in society. I feel that I was able, most of the time, to perform my work capably and with appropriate energy, knowing that it was just a part of my life, allowing erotic energy to flow, thus preserving soul in my now various life and work roles. In this middle age I experienced what Jacques called a "sculpted creativity." Less fire in the belly, but more in the stove, which can in fact warm a whole house. In those years I became Robert the Host, somewhat like Guido Calabresi when he became dean of the Yale Law School. When a reporter asked him what he wanted to do there, he said: "A friend once said to me that there are two ways of being creative: one can sing or dance, or one can create an atmosphere in which great singers and dancers can flourish. The job of a dean is to create that kind of atmosphere for students and teachers."

Phil Jackson, coach of the world champion Chicago Bulls basketball team, thinks the job of a coach is in the same mode. He writes in his book *Sacred Hoops: Spiritual Lessons of a Hardwood Warrior*, "I vowed to create an environment based on the principles of selflessness and compassion I'd learned as a Christian in my parents' home; sitting on a cushion practicing Zen; and studying the teaching of the Lakota Sioux. . . . I wanted to build a team that would blend individual talent with a heightened group consciousness. A team that could win big without becoming small in the process."

Creating an atmosphere where others may feel at home and occupy the workspace with their own talents, metaphors, and initiatives may be seen as a work of hospitality. Deans, coaches, managers, clergy, administrators, partners, and supervisors are among those whose work may bear a spirit of collegiality, in which, sometimes, conventional roles interchange in the emergence of a community in which teachers learn and students teach, patients heal and doctors are healed, clients counsel and counselors are instructed. Robert the Host also made intentional time for Robert the Father, Husband, Grandfather, Son, Brother, Friend. I was finally beginning to understand that my life is always larger than my work. I became a happier man.

In middle adulthood, how have you been holding vision open in the dark? Was there, is there a dominant work role that defines and preoccupies your life? How comfortable was or is the balance between your personal and professional lives? How have you experienced "sculpted creativity," that weathered wedding of experience and energy? In your middle years, how would you name yourself?

Re-imagining Work Life

I came towards the end of my elder passage in the fall of 1994, when at sixty-eight I retired as director of Kirkridge. Now, as I negotiate my way into the elder season, I am searching for fresh opportunities to hold vision open in the dark of society's need and my own soul. I am finding clues in the choices of some companions on the journey and invite you to consider a few of these lives in the task of *re-imagining your work life* as you make your way through the passage into the elder season.

You may want to keep on doing what you have

been doing, albeit in a more leisurely and playful manner. Attorney Charles Rembar writes:

> The thing to do about middle age is to skip it. . . . The best course is to go directly to Old. Not elderly. Not senior. Old. . . . As a lawyer, I've found Old has a huge advantage. In the bundle of talents that make a good lawyer, only one diminishes with age: the capacity to absorb a mass of facts. But that is the most boring aspect of legal work, and in Old you don't have to do it; others must suffer the boredom and hand you the product of their pain. Legal judgment and creativity are usually a matter of feeling: the glow that attends the arrival of a good idea, the slight nausea that a bad one induces. Such feeling requires recollection, conscious or not, of bygone events, of problems faced and solutions reached. . . . In court, the judge, usually younger, knows that Old has had time to develop a deeper feeling for the law than he. In addition, His Honor is acutely aware, despite the black robe and high bench, that he is not an imperious figure, but just a kid wearing a garment that may look, on him, a bit ridiculous. And so he is inclined to accept what Old so kindly explains and Old's scornful replies to his opponent's arguments. Even when Old is wrong.

As the whimsical plaque on our refrigerator has it: "Old Age and Trickery Will Overcome Youth and Ambition." If you are in one of the professions, or are an artist or a writer, or own your own business, or have a job you like that keeps on being there for you, you may choose to keep on working in some form. However, you might consider moving into the style of what I would call "playful creativity," like Charles Rembar. Relieved of the burdens of competition and ego-driven success needs, and free from conventional expectations, one might discover a gift for surprise, curiosity, and a childlike openness to the moment. After all, we have it on high authority that the only way into the kingdom of well-being is to become like a child again, but this time with all our smarts! Moving into the time of second naïveté, on the other side of cynicism.

This kind of playful creativity is embodied by coach Phil Jackson, who concludes his book with the words, "As the game unfolds, time slows down and I experience this blissful feeling of being totally engaged in the action. One moment I may crack a joke and the next cast a woeful look at a ref. But all the while I'm thinking: How many timeouts do we have left? Who needs to get going out there on the court? What's up with my guys on the bench? My mind is completely focused on the goal, but with a sense of openness and joy."

You might take a special interest in mentoring the young in your field. Journalist Barbara Jepson writes about violin teacher Dorothy Delay:

[Her] reputation as star maker and artistic midwife rests on the number of celebrated virtuosos who have studied with her—violinists like Itzhak Perlman, Shlomo Mintz, Nadja Salerno-Sonnenberg, Nigel Kennedy, Gil Shaham and Midori. . . .

Her devotion to her pupils is all-encompassing: thirty-three years ago she taught Mr. Perlman, a polio victim, how to drive a car outfitted for the handicapped; today, she oversees the activities of her latest discovery, the eleven-year-old Sarah Chang, recommending what color dresses to wear on stage and accompanying her to important concert dates. Above all, Miss Delay's goal is to stimulate pupils to listen for themselves, to heighten their awareness that there is no "correct" way to play something. "It frees their imagination," she said. In this she differs from an older generation of teachers, typically European males, who endeavored to pass on their own interpretive and stylistic ideas, sometimes in a dictatorial manner.

Dorothy Delay, a grandmotherly elder of the musical tribe, is mentoring students in her eighth decade and shudders at the thought of retirement. Others in more modest circumstances are finding ways to mentor the young with the wisdom of their mature years. Might you find such a path in your tribe?

You may choose to keep on working for social justice in the manner to which you have become accustomed. Cecelia Hellmann is a nun who has lived for over twenty years in East St. Louis, a city that became notorious for its uncollected garbage. Cecelia belongs to an international order that, writes columnist Colman McCarthy, "takes on whatever trouble God sends its way. Cecelia, now sixty-one, is in the tradition of Saul Alinsky and Mother Jones, two other

Illinois agitators who said: Don't agonize, organize."
In early 1990, she organized a group of black minis-
ters, who

> pushed the mayor and town council to form a
> trash-and-refuse commission. It also raised a stink
> when the mayor didn't include funds in the city
> budget for collection. Thirty-three people were
> arrested . . . for carrying bags of trash into city hall.
> Among those busted were clergy, teachers, and
> the elderly. . . . The demonstration and arrests
> helped focus the issue. With administrative help
> and a $360,000 commitment from the East St.
> Louis Community Fund, by year's end Operation
> New Spirit was on its way, along with the first
> piles of garbage. "It's the churches that can best
> reach local people," Cecelia believes. . . . As
> familiar with sanitation codes as with the mystery
> of her faith, Cecelia is a rare kind of environmen-
> talist. She has moved beyond dabbling in recycling
> and jumped into the trash-heap of local politics,
> demanding that politicians stop *talking* garbage in
> East St. Louis. Instead, Cecelia urges, let's get rid
> of it.

Virtually as long as we live, all kinds of people and
organizations can keep on trying to change unjust systems and structures that damage human beings and
communities. Maggie Kuhn, founder of the Gray
Panthers, died at eighty-nine. She joined striking
transit workers in Philadelphia on their picket line *two
weeks before her death*. Indeed, the elder season may
give us, if we want it, a chance to refocus our work

energies, devoting more attention to making things in society better for those who come after us. Such activity is what Erik Erikson termed "generativity." We are freer, at our age, to do what we really believe is right and good. We are, or should be, getting beyond embarrassment. In the time of what Allan Chinen, psychiatrist and author, calls "emancipated innocence" we can afford to do things like walking in a picket line or even engaging in nonviolent civil disobedience in the service of humanity and creation. After all, if we don't do it now, when will we?

We may be able to choose to keep on being productive well into our elder season, like my friend and colleague Martin Marty. Scholar, professor, senior editor of *The Christian Century*, author of forty-five books, he is a delightful and awesome reminder of the Energizer rabbit that "just keeps going and going and going." In his late sixties, he wrote in one of his columns, "I never have an unscheduled minute during weekdays. . . . Classes, seminars, student advising, meetings at three offices run from 8 A.M. to 6 P.M. How do I get reading done, since I travel every Thursday? I travel in order to get work done, on planes or late afternoons and early mornings in hotels; only my wife knows how to find me." He says that he has three or four evenings at home a month.

While I admire Marty's enormous productivity and have no doubt he is doing what he wants to do and doing it superbly well, I know that such a life and work schedule are not for me. I want to have many unscheduled hours during the week and most of my nights at home. And in addition, I want leisure and energy enough to do my own soul work, inner work that allows reading without agenda and the kind of contemplation that accompanies serious birdwatching. In other words, I want the pleasure of playing and praying and majoring in delight. William Blake wrote, "Energy is eternal delight," and in that respect Marty may have it all. But I ponder work beyond productivity, and finding that peculiar balance between doing and being that suits one's soul and season. Certainly there is joy in doing and in being, and there is the possibility of imbalance and soul damage in each. How do you assess your own balance at this time?

You may not want to keep on doing what you have been doing, or may not have the option of doing so. Forced retirement, illness, or some life change may require you to make a new life and work for yourself, like Jeannie Roth (mentioned earlier), who turned what seemed like disaster into the time of her life.

But often we have more anxiety than curiosity about what new life and work might lie out there. A friend who retired as a surgeon at seventy said to me, "I can't do just a little surgery. I have to quit it altogether. I might teach a course, but I am losing my work and it scares me. I don't want to just wait around to die." The unscheduled hours day after day can be daunting. On occasion I have found midafternoon a kind of dead time when I wonder why I'm not in some office or at some meeting. A friend was depressed after he retired, and finally found new "work" by becoming active in the life and work of his church, as well as tutoring young men on probation in the criminal justice system and participating in an "adopt a class" program at a local school. Even during an extended summer vacation he seeks out local needs, knowing that it is as good for his health as it is for the health of the community when he find a way to hold vision open in the dark of somebody's life or scene.

Sometimes you choose the work; other times the work chooses you. Dave Knapp retired in his sixties from his job as a textbook salesman to schools and other educational institutions. Previously he had been a paid executive in the Boy Scouts, and he continued that work as a volunteer in his retirement. In his fifties, Dave, married with two children, realized he was gay, and eventually was divorced. His estranged stepdaughter told local Boy Scout authorities of Dave's homosexuality, and in a gross and unkind manner he was summarily dismissed from his Scout position in the Quinnipiac Council of New Haven, Connecticut. There had been no question of any impropriety on his part over all the years of his service. It was simply against national Boy Scout policy to have homosexual people in the organization as members or leaders, and the local Scouting people felt there was nothing they could do about it. The matter received considerable publicity in the town of Guilford, Connecticut, where Dave lives and in the rest of the state as well. Newspaper and TV broadcasts referred to Dave as "Scott" in order to provide him the privacy of anonymity. The Sunday after the story broke, when the microphone was passed to those wanting to offer or request prayers in Dave's church, someone prayed for "Scott," saying that he must be going through a lot of pain and suffering. Almost unconsciously, Dave found himself asking for the mike and saying to the congregation, "I am Scott." As an usher and teacher in the church confirmation class, and a member of the church, Dave was widely respected in the congregation. After the service, people gathered around him to express support for him and anger at the Scouts' action.

When Dave came out to his congregation, it marked the first step in his *new vocation*: the work of educating people in churches, schools, and the community about homosexuality. He co-founded a support group for parents of gays and lesbians, became co-chairman of a gay/lesbian speakers association, and speaks in schools and churches across the state.

I first met Dave years before, when he attended a retreat for gay, lesbian, and bisexual people at Kirkridge. To me it is beautiful to watch how Dave has taken a humiliating and wounding affront, and made of it the text and context of his new vocation: holding vision open in the dark of our society's homophobia. His *work* now consists in sharing his *life*. He had the courage to take a big NO and turn it into a bigger and much more important YES for himself and his church and community. You and I can look for the possible yes hiding in the nos that come our way, seeking that new passion, that new dream, that new life work reaching out to tap and enlist us.

You may choose to be a volunteer in some enterprise that has long commanded your respect. If you can't think of one, you could make what I call a "Matthew Twenty-five" survey of your town and city. That's the last judgment scene (Matthew 25:31ff), in which Jesus divides the sheep and goat nations according to whether they did or did not feed the hungry, provide shelter for the naked and homeless, comfort those who mourn, visit those in prison, welcome strangers, minister to the least of these our brothers and sisters. You get the idea. Such a survey would turn up "the least of these" in your area, and you would soon find what organizations and people are doing something to help them, and even to change conditions, like Cecelia Hellmann, Maggie Kuhn, and Dave Knapp. If you want to, you can find volunteer ways to hold vision open in the dark of your time and place. A retired friend put it this way: "If you are bored in retirement, you never learned to give anything away."

We need projects that will get us out of bed in the morning eager for the day's challenges. We need to stay just a little uncomfortable. As one who loves the daily comforts and doesn't like "inconveniences," I do want to have the heart to do new things, things I could not have dreamed of considering when I had a full-time job, things that will disrupt my pleasant routine. I want to be willing to consider doing something "their way" once in a while, if it makes sense, no longer tunnel-visioned into "my way." I don't want to "collude in my own exile." I want to be newly flexible. I want the courage to take a risk now and then in the knowledge that it is risky in the elder season *not* to take risks. And above all, I want to live into the deepest, fullest humanity of which I am capable, to become, for better and for worse, Robert.

And to do that I must do my soul work. Thomas Moore writes, "The ultimate work . . . is an engagement with soul, responding to the demands of fate and tending the details of life as it presents itself. We may get to a point where our external labors and the *opus* of the soul are one and the same, inseparable. Then the satisfactions of our work will be deep and long lasting, undone neither by failures nor by flashes of success."

Passage into the elder season takes us into the primary life struggle of old age: the polarity of integrity and despair, in Erikson's terms. I have had to learn, with some pain, that it isn't a matter of integrity *or* despair but integrity *and* despair. We will wrestle with both the rest of our lives, and and have to discover again and again that only in engaging despair and embracing sorrow can we make our way into some measure of integrity and joy.

Soul work involves welcoming all the fear, disappointment, tragedy, and remorse of your life into the house, letting them take their places at your table, along with the hope, fulfillment, grace, and gratitude of your years. Soul work involves embracing what has happened to you, bad and good, as somehow acceptable, somehow bearable if not explainable in the strange mystery of life and death. Soul work involves gathering in the meanings of your life, circling around to touch bases important to you, day by day, year by year. It includes remembering important events and people, consciously reweaving the gorgeous tear-stained threads of your colorful life into a fresh tapestry of meaning.

The people and places of your visitation in memory and in touch will recapitulate your unique story. Your soul work will necessarily, painfully, and delightfully breathe the color, taste, and individuality of your life. And as you go about this work, you may come to a fresh face-to-face encounter with yourself, as the singular human being emerging out of your history. As Rembrandt painted his self-portrait year by year, you may, year by year, recognize more of your soul in your face. William Stringfellow, attorney and theologian, wrote, "I am called in the Word of God to be William Stringfellow, nothing more, nothing less." Who can tell what William or *you* will do? There is a sacred unpredictability about us older ones, an inviolable eccentricity that is to be valued by us if not always by others! Wendell Berry, in another poem, sounds our clarion call:

So, friends, every day do something
that won't compute. Love the Lord.
Love the world. Work for nothing.

Love someone who does not deserve it.
Denouce the government and embrace
 the flag.

Ask the questions that have no answers.
Invest in the millennium. Plant sequoias.

Put your faith in the two inches of humus
 that will build under the trees
 every thousand years.

Expect the end of the world. Laugh.
Laughter is immeasurable. Be joyful
 though you have considered all the facts.

Practice resurrection.

Part of who you are is who you will be.

As we review and re-imagine our work life, making our way towards the elder season, harvest time approaches: time for gathering in the fruits of our labors, for savoring what is good and letting the rest go. There will be other harvest times in the years ahead, but many of us need to come to terms with the fact that our major work contribution has probably been made. While we may be able to add richly to it, there it is today, for better and for worse. We can accept it with all its disappointments and delights, its achievements and frustrations, taking comfort in the truth that our work doesn't define us or exhaust the meaning of our life.

And yet no leaf or grain is filled
By work of ours; the field is tilled
And left to grace. That we may reap
Great work is done while we're asleep.

Some kind of partnership is going on. There is surely the partnership of the generations. As others prepared the ground for us, even now others are coming along to take up the common work of holding vision open in the dark. Our responsibility, like our time and energy, is finite. But more, you and I are partners with One who is always doing the Great Work of the universe. Augustine wrote, "God has a work to do with us that will not be done without us." Matthew Fox writes in his book *The Re-invention of Work* that "the new cosmology" teaches us . . . there is only one work going on in the universe, the 'Great Work' of creation unfolding, the work of evolution or creativity in the universe. The poet Rilke speaks of 'the great work' and of the gap we feel in our work lives, cut off as we are from the Great Work:

> For somewhere there is an ancient enmity
> between our daily life and the great work.
> Help me, in saying it, to understand it.

Just being able to name the reality of a Great Work in the universe has the power to restore our dignity and to restore dignity to our work. The last line of this passage from Rilke also contains a kind of *prayer*, the hint of a personal *presence* in the universe that attends to our honest yearning to understand. The Great Work is the Great Mystery."

However you are apprehended by the Great Mystery, your work is not lost, but plays its own modest but indispensable part in the ongoing unfolding and healing of creation. The field of the family is tilled and left to grace. Your parenting, grandparenting, uncleing, aunting, brothering, sistering, befriending, mentoring are left to grace. You hope and pray in your way for those you love, and leave them all to grace. The field of the nations and the planet is tilled and left to grace, "unto the seventh generation." You commit small daily acts of courage, and demonstrate hope while entrusting all to grace.

I love those words "Great work is done while we're asleep." When I wake at night fearful for myself or my children or others known or unknown to me who are in danger or trouble, I repeat those words and entrust them to the One who neither slumbers nor sleeps, the One who keeps on preserving our going out and our coming in. It doesn't mean we or they are protected from tragedy, which happens every day and night, or from foolish choices made by us or others, or from chance or accident. But it does mean that our "Partner in the field" is working and that we may entrust all we hold dear to that faithful Worker. We may sow our work and our very lives into the ground of the earth, in hope of a gracious harvest beyond our vision and our death. The doctrine of the restoration of all things declares that nothing is lost, everything is vulnerable to recovery, transformation. There is word about the resurrection of the body and a new creation, yielding hope that not just our souls but our embodied selves, our bodysouls, the creation itself is in process of being changed, and who knows what is being prepared for the homecoming of all being. We're not the only ones imagining work.

When we work well, a Sabbath mood
Rests on our day, and finds it good.

These last lines constitute a kind of benediction. The late Bart Giamatti, president of Yale University and later commissioner of baseball (in the time when they had *real* commissioners), wrote a delightful little book called *Take Time for Paradise*. He wrote of leisure as nonwork activity that is chosen for its own sake, with a festive sensibility, like art or sport or learning, carefree in its own delight, like children or lovers at play. Such moments of leisure and pure pleasure, he said, "transcend notions of accountability taking us into a state of radiant contemplation."

Giamatti's coda leads us beautifully into the consideration of love, which we will explore in the next chapter as the fifth task of creative aging—nurturing intimacy.

Questions for pondering:

What are your retirement issues?

If you could write your own work description, what would it look like?

What institutions or causes energize you and call you to offer your volunteer time and care?

Are you interested in letting yourself lie fallow for a while, waiting for a signal from your soul or an external invitation or challenge?

What soul work do you want or need to do?

5· Nurturing Intimacy

But that other;
he danced like a gypsy's bear at the winter crossroads,
the days of your youth and his are a bit of blue glass
bevelled by oceans and kept in his pocket,
wherever he is is always
now.
Touch, mass, weight, warmth:
a language you found you knew.
He brought you
the bread of sunlight on great platters of laughter.

—Denise Levertov

At the "winter crossroads" of the elder passage, we are not svelte antelopes or nubile gazelles, but "dancing bears": shaggy, festive, graceful, Teddy grown old, young love remembered, old love savored, new love found or awaited or let go. We are our own gypsy masters, presenting ourselves for our own pleasure and the delight of others. The language of love that we found we knew can never be forgotten, though if it is not spoken for a while, it may seem hidden in reticence.

Who is it now, at the winter crossroads between middle age and the elder season, that brings you "the bread of sunlight on great platters of laughter"? Your lover, spouse, or partner may feed your hunger of body and soul with rich, dark bread and dry vintage wine, chasing away the shadows with the yellow light of afternoon, presenting you with laughing delight. Or it may be your niece or grandchild or sister or friend who lights up your life. The garment of intimacy is woven with many threads, each providing a lifeline of comfort, security, belonging, and trust.

In the thirteenth chapter of Matthew, Jesus tells twin parables about seeking and finding, which give us clues in our consideration of intimacy:

> The kingdom of heaven is like treasure hidden in a field, which someone found and hid; then in his joy he goes and sells all that he has and buys that field.
>
> Again, the kingdom of heaven is like a merchant in search of fine pearls; on finding one pearl of great value, he went and sold all that he had and bought it.

If we think of intimacy as treasure of great value, so precious that we would give all that we have to obtain it, we realize that sometimes we seek it with great intentionality, in this relationship or that, pursuing it, even obsessed with finding and possessing it. Though we may try to ferret it out, our efforts are often futile.

There is a mystery and a privacy and a grace about intimacy, which seems to hide itself from direct pursuit. Rather, it seems to make its presence or possibility known indirectly, by surprise. We stumble upon it by accident as though fate had chosen us to find the treasure. But in truth intimacy bears the quality of revelation in which we see ourselves brilliantly anew from within and discover quite serendipitously that we are there for another, and that other for us—the moment laden with potential. Finding and being found by such intimacy may enlarge our capacity for joy. It may change and disrupt our lives. It may take all we have to enjoy it.

According to the parables, the treasure (of intimacy) may be found by *intention* or *attention*. Surely that is true to our experience. Yet it may also be the case that, at our age, attention—curiosity, openness of heart and mind, sensitivity to the souls of others, and a capacity to wait—may better suit the season.

Helen Stark Tomkins, a friend and wise woman in her late seventies, rich in relationships and experience, writes: "I think 'seeking intimacy' is best realized through living to the fullest all that we are capable of and by trusting that the more we give of ourselves in the search to understand the nature of reality and our rightful place in the universe as a whole, the more attractive we become to others on the same planet. Judging by St. Francis's experience, this probably applies as well to kingdoms other than what we call 'human' . . . i.e., 'I hold my love but lightly. . . . Things with wings will want to fly away.' "

As we find intimacy in a variety of relationships and modes, we want to cultivate and nurture it, which is the fifth task of our passage. Let us consider the variety of our circumstances, conditions, needs, wants, and choices regarding intimacy.

Being Single

Ina Hart, a pastor in her late fifties, wrote:

I never achieved intimacy in my marriage, and am not secure in my ability to do so. As far as men are concerned, I'm still waiting. But I'm learning something in my single life. The self I'm discovering is very important to me. Being that self isn't an either/or thing, and any marriage I might enter into would have to include this self. I think that's my new definition of intimacy—being *myself* and being enjoyed, while I offer space to a partner in the same way. The intimacy I now enjoy is pastoring a small congregation and being honest and personal with the people and in my preaching. I am finally learning to confront issues head-on. Also I have several great relationships with women friends. After dinner with a Roman Catholic priest friend recently, I realized how much I enjoy a male friendship where the sex issue has already been settled. My insecurity may be related to sex and how to have a dialogue which includes it. I feel terribly gauche. Also I haven't yet come across anyone who is unpartnered. So I am waiting to risk being open and aware of the possibility that an intimate friendship might occur, including even sexual expression. But I'm not moving from my small town or joining any groups. If such a relationship happens, the other person will have to be equally open to risk, as well as secure in remaining alone.

Ina knows who she is, has a deep sense of self-esteem, and has lived into an individuality that is uniquely hers, which is her treasure and which she will offer to another only when that other approaches her in the same way. She has a clear sense of her own boundaries and a rich understanding of intimacy as two selves enjoying each other in mutually offered space. She is living now a mature single life, with various intimate connections, and should she marry in the future, she would seek a mature interdependence, founded on healthy independence. She is willing to risk a new relationship, as well as to remain alone.

Betty Friedan writes of the "rage" that she and other single older women feel about the unavailability of male partners. There are 5.3 times as many widows as widowers; 77 percent of men over sixty-five are married, while only 38 percent of women over sixty-five are married. Men who are widowed or divorced typically choose younger women to marry or to live with. In the gay community, aging men are often regarded as less attractive sexual partners, though AIDS has fostered more intense and sustained friendship among single and partnered gay men of all ages. The lesbian community is more welcoming to unpartnered women, straight as well as lesbian, and provides a network of relationships, some of which are sexual, others not. AIDS has brought gay men, lesbians, and some heterosexual people closer in mutual sorrow and care, affording many relationships with the other sex that are deeply intimate, yet not explicitly sexual.

One may find oneself in a situation similar to Ina's, content with an independent lifestyle, settled into a comfortable autonomy, not seeking sexual intimacy, but willing to risk being open to it should the possibility arise. Or one may long for a sexual partner. Marjorie, a divorced woman in her late fifties, wrote, "The discussion about intimacy in the workshop was painful; I haven't had a sexual partner in sixteen years."

George, a widower in his mid-seventies, has chosen not to get married but to relate to a number of women, some of the relationships being sexual, others not. He says he enjoys the company of women and finds that sexual intimacy provides the context for sharing his deepest personal feelings. He prefers a network of close relationships to having a primary partner.

Ann, a divorced woman of independent means in her late fifties, chose to live in a seaside town in Florida for many years, enjoying relationships with young lovers and an easy lifestyle. Now, she says, she is ready for some measure of commitment in a long-term relationship. I am reminded of Maggie Kuhn, who had an affair with a man in his twenties when she was in her seventies, and of the character Maude in the film *Harold and Maude*, who, as an older woman, taught the young man Harold about life and love. When he said to her in wonder, "You're so good with people," she replied, "They're my species, you know." One gift of age often is the ability to be good with people. Another is the ability to be comfortable living as an eccentric, unfettered, open-to-the-world person who can evoke the capacity for intimacy in another. At our age we can live and give the gift of emancipated innocence.

My friend Jane, sixty-five, a retired professional

woman, divorced for many years, says, "I am not interested in an intimate sexual relationship; I don't want ever again to be that vulnerable." She is an exuberant woman who has warm friendships with many men and women, and has chosen to become part of a close-knit retirement community. For her, celibacy in the elder season is a glad and life-giving choice. While she declines sexual intimacy, she revels in the emotional intimacy she experiences with family and friends.

At our age, and in our age, we are free to make intimacy choices, perhaps for the first time as adults. Some of us were virgins when we first got married, and followed a conventional pattern of sexual relationship. Our choices were narrowly defined, unlike those presented to Mary Catherine Bateson, daughter of famed anthropologists Gregory Bateson and Margaret Mead: "I was offered many lifestyles: marriage with children or marriage without children, marriage open or faithful, transient or sustained, home-making or an outside career, solitude or commitment, the love of men or the love of women." She writes of her mother: "Appreciating individual diversity almost as a connoisseur appreciates works of art, and bringing me into relationship with a range of people who had made profoundly different choices and represented different ways of being human, different ways of constructing family life, different ways of being a woman . . . [she] taught me to perceive and value differences and accentuate them as interesting in themselves, rather than as deviations from the ideal." We now have the opportunity to become

connoisseurs of intimacy in our relationships of choice
at this time in our lives.

Partners

What shall we say about partnered intimacy, especially for persons on the elder journey? I was required
to think about this when invited to celebrate the
marriage of a widower and a divorced woman in their
late fifties. What I came up with was a piece I titled
"Charge to the Couple." While part of my "charge"
was particular to this couple's circumstances, most of
the material was pertinent to other couples. In addition, the form of the "charge" distilled my hopes
for them, for my wife and me, and for other mature
couples, offering a set of clues to finding and nurturing the treasure of partnered intimacy in the elder
passage. Here is how it went:

I commend to you Rilke's words on marriage:

> "as the love that consists in this: two
> solitudes bordering, protecting,
> and saluting each other."
> May you nourish each other's solitude
> and your own, that your selfhood may
> remain clear and strong,
> that what you share may be deep
> and fresh.
> As mature human beings, you do not enter today
> into a merger
> but a partnership
> in which there shall be equality of status and power,

in which the autonomy of each is respected
and the accountability of each required.

As you join two separate family systems,
with the felicities and fallibilities of each,
may you welcome your new families
with respect for their traditions
even as you honor your own,
with a willingness to tolerate eccentricities
even as you recognize your own.
There is risk in what you commit here today,
for nothing is guaranteed.
But there is also great promise,
for everything, with God, is possible.
You have lived long enough to expect unconditional
love from no one.
Therefore, may you be granted the grace
to forbear and forgive much,
to laugh and cry together,
to comfort and confront each other,
to delight in one another's joys,
and bear one another's sorrows.

A marriage needs equal portions of
passion and patience.
As companions, lovers, and friends,
may you discover and celebrate
the ways of intimacy natural to each and both.
The gift of erotic longing enables you to become
vulnerable to each other in moments of
tenderness, self-revelation, and gratitude.
Intimacy consists in the capacity and willingness
of self-revelation and of receiving

the self-revelation of the other.
Intimacy is born out of the sharing of privacies,
    and flourishes in a context of trust.
May you be laughers as well as listmakers together,
    creating an ease and lightness of being
    in which safety and freedom abide.

May you live into a quiet communion, in which, as
Robert Bly writes,

   "A man and a woman sit near each other, and they
        do not long at this moment to be older, or
     younger, nor born in any other nation, time or
       place. They are content to be where they are,
                talking or not talking."

And remember, you do not walk alone.
You are surrounded by a cloud of witnesses,
    families and friends here gathered,
    others not now present,
    and some who have gone before you.
We all have a stake in your marriage.
Your happiness is important to us.
Count on us to walk with you,
and entrust yourselves to the One who has brought
    you
across rivers of grief, through forests of uncertainty
  to this day of great hope.

William Blake gives you this send-off:

            "He who binds to himself a joy
            Doth the winged life destroy;

But he who kisses the joy as it flies
Lives in eternity's sunrise."

May you keep on kissing the joy!

But how do you keep on "kissing the joy" in times of routine and boredom, anger and hurt, or disruptions in work or in the lives of those you love? How do you deal with the process of habituation that screens out the novel and stimulating, or with the burden of aging bodies—conditions that afflict all long-term partnerships? A friend in his mid-sixties put it this way: "Much current literature tends to talk in glowingly positive terms about sex in the elder years—a welcome swing of the pendulum. But at least in the books and articles I've read I find little that deals forthrightly with how we adjust ourselves to issues of maintaining an enjoyable and satisfying sex life in the face of any or all of the common experiences of declining desire, arthritis, bad backs, colostomies, menopause, sweaty hot flashes, vaginal discomforts of one kind or another, impotence, etc. etc. Hopefully, no couples will have to contend with all of these at once! However, I suspect most couples have to deal with at least one, and probably more, sometimes for the long haul, and that any or all of these can be inhibitors, or even preventers, of activities which had become very satisfying and meaningful aspects of intimacy."

I note that my friend, in his recital of conditions inhibiting or preventing intimacy, mentioned last that most fearsome of conditions to men, impotence. The good news is that, while some older men will have to abide this condition without improvement, most will find remedies in therapy or in medication, penile implants, self-injection with vasoactive drugs, or some other treatment. Men are coming out of the impotence closet and learning that they are not alone or bizarre in their difficulty, that most men experience periods of moderate impotence, and that there is much that can be done about it. The expert word today is that for men over fifty-five impotence is more often physiological than emotional in origin, and therefore subject to physiological remedies. A man's first experiences of what author Aaron Kipnis prefers to call "diminished erotic response" can be devastating. Mine certainly were. Being a religious type, I found my prayer life escalating during that period. My basic prayer was: "Lord, strike me if you must, but not there!" In due course, with the understanding encouragement of my wife and consultation with a psychiatrist and urologist, my erotic response returned, most of the time, to normal. I am trying to become a non-anxious lover, accepting whatever turn-on occurs, and enjoying the leisurely pleasures of "getting there," which may indeed be half the fun of the mutual journey. We need to let go of our inhibitions and give our erotic imaginations a chance, allowing ourselves freedom to "play" together in whatever ways are mutually pleasurable.

Is there a new paradigm for sexual intimacy in the elder season? I think there is. It has in part to do with lovemaking as leisurely playtime. If foreplay has received deserved good press, and the play is the thing, afterplay also deserves its time in the sunlight of bread and wine and laughter. After the urgencies are released comes the time of gentle glances, gestures, words, caresses. Couples create their own private rituals of intimacy, their own ways of honoring, thanking, and pleasuring one another. The more years we enjoy what Wendell Berry calls "the sweetness of ripening," the deeper and more lovely may be our delight in one another and the more able we may become to enter what Betty Friedan terms "a further stage in intimacy," beyond preoccupation with "penetration and phallic intercourse," in which truth-telling and closeness cohere.

She writes of a man in his late sixties, who after forty years of marriage experienced the most profound loving and touching and knowing of his wife after she was diagnosed with inoperable cancer: "I told her, whatever happens, I promise to tell you the truth, to keep nothing from you. . . . Those were the most joyous, the most wonderful months of my life, with all the pain and horror . . . , [our] being completely open like that. I thought we had a good marriage before, . . . [but s]uddenly we were there, that incredible strong thing between us, and I really knew what she was feeling, and she really knew me."

That couple lived a new paradigm of partnered intimacy, centering on truth-telling, being completely open, and savoring the shining moments in the midst of pain and sorrow. In their "good marriage" they were never so intimate as in the dying time, when they found their souls becoming as naked as their bodies. Those who have lost partners by death, divorce, or departure have the gift of intimate memories, which may be honored even as they find their appropriate places in the rich history of our relationships.

For some couples, some of the time, it is as though everything one does is intimate, whether in the gathering of wildflowers, the momentary glance at the dining table, being in different rooms of the house, simply being aware of the other, with gratitude, amazed that you have found your way through all the vicissitudes to live gladly together in this place. But not always gladly. Angry words sometimes fill the air and help to clear it; there can be no honest intimacy without expression of the anger that arises in every partnership, which, acknowledged and processed, allows healing to take place. Laughter erupts with the timely repetition of inside jokes, the ludicrous habits noted, the endless, marvelous funniness generated by each and both.

Intimacy without laughter would seem to me sober and dull, though there may also be a courtliness, a self-restraint, as expressed by writer Loren Eiseley:

Here on my window ledge
                    two cardinals,
                    male and female,
having lived alone all winter
          in that silence of the solitary
                    who seek their own food
                    and depend on no one,
suddenly exchange seeds
               in an ancient ritual
               welcoming spring.
They are not too intimate,
                    the horn of the beak preventing.
                    They are very wild

but grave and dignified—
>   at this moment
so much so that if I could
>   with the proper manners
I should like to give
>   a seed to you.

I have witnessed that ancient cardinal ritual dozens of times at our feeders, and it never fails to delight me. It constitutes a living parable of two solitudes bordering, protecting, and saluting each other. It is the grave and dignified wildness of their exchange that causes me to nod my head in creaturely recognition.

Family Connections

Beyond partnered relationships, the horizon of our intimate connections stretches out generously to include a range of family members. Thomas Moore writes: "The family the soul wants is a felt network of relationship, an evocation of a certain kind of interconnection that grounds, roots, nestles. . . . It always provides a fundamental relatedness that doesn't depend upon attraction or compatibility. People working on a project together, for example, may feel the presence of family as they talk, work, and get to know each other. When we hope that our nation can hold together as a family, or that the family of nations can live in peace, these are not metaphors, but rather the expressions of a profound need of the soul for a special grounded way of relating that offers deep, unconditional, and lasting security."

We are both blessed and cursed with our own

families. One may have needed to divest oneself of one's family in order to survive, or one may have grown remote by reason of death, distance, divorce, hurt, anger, indifference. But now in our later years, we may consider trying to recover and restore relationships with various members of our family.

My siblings provide increasing comfort to me, though not without bumps along the road. My brother John and I jointly own cottages on a hill overlooking a lake in Michigan. For fourteen years now, we have sought to steward our property wisely, exercising joint authority in making choices regarding needed repairs, and sharing equally in the financial cost of it all. Several years ago, an issue arose around which we had serious disagreement. We consulted lawyers, argued, agreed to disagree, and maintained a tight-lipped silence about the issue, trying not to let it damage our relationship. A few months later John and his family were at our house for a New Year's party. Late the first night we thrashed through the matter again, winding up in a tense impasse. The next afternoon, we took a walk in the woods, and while we were walking, a way opened towards a common place where each of us could stand his ground in mutual acceptance. I felt warmth from my brother and tenderness towards him. Our battle of opposing convictions yielded a tiny flow of grace. A moment of intimacy was born from honest combat.

Neither of us wanted to let this thing drive a permanent wedge between us. I think each of us believed that our relationship was strong enough to be honest about our feelings and convictions, and that somehow we would find our way to an acceptable resolution.

We did, and are closer than before because of what we went through together. Anger can sometimes be the friend of intimacy in a family relationship where both parties to a quarrel care enough to hang on until a mutually agreeable solution emerges. Sometime later, I wrote my thoughts about the encounter in the form of a prayer: "Lord, quiet our sibling fears and soften our suspicions. Let the soil of our heritage, now ploughed up, be fertile ground for fresh hope. Let hard bargaining yield more than justice and reach beyond accommodation towards the magnanimity of those who have walked the narrow edge of separation, and been saved, this time, from stumbling over the precipice. Let your tenderness yearn over us."

There is special delight in the light-touch relationships possible with one's nieces and nephews. I find myself, in these years, wanting to connect more deeply with these young people, who enrich my life and will take our family heritage into the future along with my own children. Uncles and aunts have opportunities to befriend, unencumbered by heavy parental agendas or sibling rivalries. When my daughter Nancy was married, my brother Dick sent her a monetary gift, as he had done for my daughter Cathy and step-daughter Sally when each of them was married. But this time he also sent a similar check to my single daughter Barb, not wanting to leave her out of his largesse. It was a lovely surprise, nurturing the tie between Dick and Barb, and delighting me as well. I notice that Dick, perhaps in part because he does not have children of his own, is very intentional about tending relationships with his nieces and nephews. They are important to him, and so he has become important to them. At my stepson Matt's wedding, his uncle Brad, learning that the wedding party was making up a purse to enable Matt and his bride, strapped by a limited budget, to take a honeymoon, gave a generous check to the fund, on top of a wedding gift already made. Though Brad and Matt had not seen each other in several years, and might not see each other again for years to come, that little gesture will be remembered with delight by both of them. An intimate deposit in the memory bank.

Grandparents are often able to develop and enjoy close relationships with grandchildren. Some occasions have to be created or responded to, such as birthdays, holidays, special occasions like a recital or ball game, or a good grade, or starting kindergarten. Other occasions just happen. One night while visiting my children I was to sleep in grandson Kyle's room and in his bed, he on an air mattress nearby in the room. When I came up to bed he was fast asleep. I looked at the dear little boy, loving him, and lay in bed delighting in this serendipitous privilege of sleeping in the same room with my grandson. Towards morning Kyle awoke and asked me if he might get in bed with me. I said, "Sure"; and so we slept a few more hours, side by side. A bit of treasure stumbled upon, a precious occasion of being close.

Relationships with one's children seem likely to continue as they have been, for better or for worse, unless some special initiative is taken to change course. Some women may have especially problematic relationships with daughters. David Dodson Gray wrote me: "This seems acute, and is experienced by the elder women as rejection, when the daughter has found her mother not to be someone she could emulate and admire as a role model of how a grown woman lives a good and fulfilling life. It is difficult to have your grown daughter turn away from you because you aren't what she wants herself to be. . . . Many women I know are turning away from those painful and attenuated relationships with daughters and now forging fiercely autonomous lives of their own. The relationships they count on are with peers and with nonfamily younger women with whom they do not have this bad history and who can see them fresh and new as older women they can admire, enjoy, and learn from and even see as older mentors and models. They care a lot less about what their daughters may think of them now than they did when they were early into the elder passage."

Homing places often provide a context or matrix of family intimacy. It may be a living room, kitchen, or dining room, wherever the family hangs out when together for special occasions. Photo albums picture you and other family members down the years in that same room, with that same furniture and those same pictures on the wall. Some who were there in older pictures are now gone, other new faces appear, and so the room gathers and holds the family soul in its generous and problematic space.

In my family the porch of the lake cottage is a matrix of intimacy. I sit on this porch where four generations of our family have taken vacations over a period of forty-six years. It is screened in; a fading braided rug covers part of the dark wooden floor; there is a creaky swing at one end, a day bed at the other, two caned highback rockers, window flowerboxes crammed with petunias whose flowers are pink or blue and yellow or purple and white. This porch is a marker place where the past year may be mulled over and the year to come imagined. It is a reviewing stand where in intimate memory I watch my parents, siblings, children, and stepchildren, and their partners and children and friends, passing by. Here I see us again at the family funerals, weddings, graduations, anniversaries, birthdays, baptisms. Every year is, of necessity, a vintage year; every holiday a holy day. I sit alone, but there are voices and faces all around.

Friendship

If we want to tend the hearth of our family soul and to keep its fires bright and warm, we also want to nurture those friends who are vital members of our intimate circle, our wider family. We call a special friend "brother" or "sister." We say to someone close to us "You're like family to me." Thomas Moore writes: "Friendship doesn't ask for a great deal of activity, but it does require loyalty and presence. After all, what the soul wants is attachment—a detached friendship is a contradiction in terms. Therefore, like all forms of soulful living, friendship demands attention. We may be present to our friend through visits, phone calls, letters, or postcards. . . . Some of my most treasured tokens of friendship are postcards with only a half-sentence on them, best if the half-sentence is thoughtful, or if it conjures up some intimacy between me and the sender. I have a treasured postcard from James Hillman that reads simply, 'My health? Root canal and spreading bad poison ivy, and yours?' "

I am reminded of the postcards that Douglas Steere, during his eighties, would send my wife and me from time to time, covering in fine print the whole of the card, and usually scribbling almost illegible final thoughts along the edges. Douglas, who died at ninety-two, was professor of philosophy at Haverford College for decades, mentor of hundreds of students and younger colleagues, and an irenic generator of interfaith friendship and conversation, literally all over the world. He came into my life when I was in my thirties, and generously welcomed me as a young colleague, offering me opportunities of relationship and experience otherwise out of my reach, quietly mentoring me on my spiritual journey, without laying any agenda upon me. When my wife and I went to Kirkridge, he and his wife, Dorothy, led retreats now and then, encouraging our work and supporting it every year financially. They had a cottage in Michigan, a few hours away from ours, and each summer for several years we would rendezvous for lunch halfway between to catch up. In between these visits came the occasional postcard. I realize now, even more than when Douglas was alive, what a blessed friend he was to us and to so many others. Just knowing he was out there cheering us on was a comfort. The last time we saw him was in the retirement community where he and Dorothy had an apartment. Though he could not then speak clearly because of a debilitating illness, by gesture, glance, and touch he conveyed his affection for us. I always felt secretly that I wasn't quite worthy of this great human being's friendship, and yet all the time his friendship was conferring worth on me, and my own capacity for friendship was being enlarged by being the beneficiary of his.

An intimate friend is a treasure one doesn't want to lose, but I did lose some over the busy decades of my preoccupation with work and family. One friend I lost, and found again, is Dale Liechty. We met and became buddies in the Navy in the Second World War, were roommates in college, and participated in each other's weddings. We lived in different parts of the country and seldom saw each other. Our lives moved apart: he became a busy surgeon, I a busy minister, and we stopped writing each other. We connected again, gladly but carefully, at our fortieth college reunion and began to correspond occasionally. Then at our forty-fifth college reunion, my wife and I, now living just a few miles from our college, set up a dinner gathering. It was such a joy to me to have Dale and his wife in our home, to touch base personally and warmly after all the years of silent absence, and to recover and restore the soul of our friendship of fifty years. We may not see one another often in the future, but I am thankful to have rekindled the warmth of our friendship, preserving our history of intimate memory.

A college or high-school reunion presents a structured opportunity to consider what friends one wants to reach out to and possibly recover. I learned this too late for my high-school graduating class. I went to my fiftieth reunion, the first one I had attended, and found that while it was good to see some former friends, there was no longer opportunity to do the work required for restoring those friendships. The years of our friendship were too remote—I had waited too long.

I have more time and energy now in retirement for nurturing old friendships and cultivating new ones. But more important, I realize I *want* and *need* friends more than when I was younger. This may be characteristic of men in our society, as Morton Hunt suggests in his article "About Men—The Age of Intimacy." He writes:

How is it that after having been friends for 20 or 30 years (and in some cases much longer) we are only now becoming intimate? We're all older men, but not yet aged. . . . But because we've all recently lost other friends and some of us now have ailments that are likely to end our lives, we have become keenly aware of our mortality. Somehow this has made it possible, perhaps even necessary, for us to convey feelings spontaneously and reveal ourselves to one another as we have not in all the years of our youth and middle age. . . . My oldest friend was widowed three years ago. A couple of months later he came to visit; when we talked about his wife, he wept openly and unashamedly, the first time I had seen him do that in a lifetime. Later we talked about whether he would eventually look for another mate, and he said that while he felt a great need for companionship, he could never love again; it would be a betrayal of his dead wife. Then he added, "To tell the truth, I'd be afraid to get involved with anyone, because I had no sex all the years she was sick and I don't know if I could make it. . . . I doubt that I could." A year later he was confiding in me about his feelings for a new woman in his life and how incredible he finds it that he can love—and make love—again. . . . How fortunate that we can be intimate now, when we need to be. How sad that we never could before.

Intimate friendship in age is a matter of exchanging vulnerabilities and savoring opportunities to know and be known more deeply. I take special delight in the friendship shared over forty-six years with summer vacation neighbors on that hillside overlooking the lake. Along with Barbara Schilling (formerly Harris) and her family mentioned earlier, friends Tom and Mary Rodman and their children and grandchildren are the other family on the hill, right next door to us. Over the decades we have all settled into an easy and abiding friendship, having suffered the early death of children, divorces, the suicide of a loved one, the deaths of our parents, and all the weddings and births, watching the children and grandchildren grow up, catching up year after year on the dock. We have threatened each other with writing a spicy book about the "secret lives" of the hillside families titled *On the Dock*. But in fact we all have been writing that book in our hearts year by year and know it and each other by heart.

Arrogance, insecurity, fear of incurring obligation, or sheer weariness may keep us from accepting invitations from, or making them to, new people in our life. Friedan writes: "We must continually beware of our own tendency to try to repeat—or defend against— ways of loving that sustained or betrayed us in youth, retreating behind self-erected walls of isolation or frantic public activity to avoid rejection, humiliation, instead of risking, risking, risking the reality of intense, shared, intimate experience."

Four words sum up, for me, the soul and substance of intimate friendship: *affection, comfort, knowing,* and *delight.* Mutual affection warms and gladdens the heart; comfort lies in the knowledge that you care for one another and will be there for one another; knowing and being known yields the security of a mutual respect that abides; delight consists in the tasty bread and vintage wine of relationship together.

Strangers

Intimacy across barriers of diversity with "the other" may elude us as we age, unless we take those rare opportunities for such encounter when they come to us, and risk the unknown. Our friends Jim and Wilys Claire Nelson live in Minneapolis, where they have participated over the years in efforts to secure civil and religious rights for gay, lesbian, and bisexual people. Two of their many gay friends were Bob and Bill, both suffering from AIDS and Bill nearing death. Jim writes:

> A few months before Bill died, he and Bob phoned us one Sunday afternoon. On that particular day, my wife's eighty-two-year-old mother was visiting us. Coming from a lifetime in small-town South Dakota, she had never knowingly even met a gay man. Bob and Bill were phoning to say that they would like to drop in with some bran muffins and brownies they had just baked.

We told Mother they were coming. She had known from our previous mention of these friends that they were gay. Before they arrived, we told her, in addition, that they both had AIDS and that Bill did not have much longer to live. We felt it important to tell her that, for Bill would clearly show the ravages of his illness—the racking cough from pneumocystis, the lesions of Kaposi's sarcoma, the wasted body. She deserved the opportunity to be prepared.

They came. We were not sure what Mother's reaction would be. . . . When they entered the living room, Mother did not remain seated, though her age would have justified it. She got out of her chair and went to greet them, extending her hand. The five of us visited for an hour or so. Bill and Bob then departed, leaving their gift of bran muffins and brownies. Soon after they left, we three sat down for a light Sunday evening supper. Their gifts of food were on the table along with a few other things from the refrigerator. With all the common fears about AIDS transmission in the public mind, we did not know what Mother would eat. The conversation centered around their visit. She wanted to know more about these two men, and finally said, "I'm really glad I was here to meet your friends." Then, rather deliberately, "I believe I'll have one of those bran muffins." She ate two, and finished with a brownie, as did each of us. Never before or since has the Sacrament been more real to me: the broken bread coming from Christ's broken bodies—and giving life. . . . Both Bill and Bob are now dead, but they were bearers of grace. They still are.

And so is Jim's mother-in-law, a woman of age who had the courage and imagination to risk intimate connection with strangers. There are moments when the ordinary suddenly becomes extraordinary, and we notice that the ground on which we are standing is holy. We cannot summon or seek such encounters, because they are always grace-given, but we can choose to open ourselves to welcome "the other," knowing that sometimes the unknown yields fresh beauty and truth.

Place

In these years I have come to feel intimately connected to the small pond one hundred feet down the hill from our house. Vine Deloria Jr., a Native American theologian, said that when his people say "nature" they mean the immediate surroundings, the creek you live on, the valley or Sacred Mountain that forms the center of your universe—all the relations that life-forms have in a specific place. In springtime, if I wake up in the middle of the night, I have a hard time getting back to sleep—what with the alto saxophone blast of bullfrogs crying out for love. Wood duck and mallard couples feed and look for nesting places. Green herons stalk the shores in summertime, pouncing every few minutes to feast on a tadpole. There are turtles, minnows, hordes of surface insects on the water, and of course, mosquitoes. Occasionally a broad-shouldered hawk resident in our woods will swoop down on some rodent or tadpole, and bluebirds fight with sparrows for a nesting house.

I feel affection for the pond and its creatures. It invites me to belong to this particular place and allows me to be a neighbor. It draws forth my soul. I am grateful to the pond and feel responsible to preserve its health in whatever ways I can. It turns my personal affection into political concern. Brother Sun, Sister Moon, Cousin Pond, Grandfather Mountain. Maria Jose Hobday is a Ute Indian and Franciscan sister. One day when she was a child her mother spoke to her as they stood before Sleeping Ute Mountain. "Take this beauty into your heart," she urged, "learn it. Someday you will only be able to see this with the eyes of your heart. Then it will be important for you to have the beauty inside you. Memorize the land." What is the land or water you have learned by heart?

Community

All our intimacies pour into the pool of community, each fresh experience sending widening circles across the water as deep calls to deep. Whether we share ourselves with lovers, family members, friends, strangers, or nature, we are adding to the storehouse of our intimate memories. Whatever our occasions of intimacy, we sense that we are being apprehended by the holy. Our small rituals of love and praise participate in the endless liturgy of creation.

In her novel *Beloved*, Toni Morrison tells the story of Baby Suggs, a woman who

> decided that, because slave life had 'busted her legs, back, head, eyes, hands, kidneys, womb and tongue,' she had nothing left to make a living with but her heart—which she put to work at once. Accepting no title of honor before her name, but

allowing a small caress after it, she became an unchurched preacher, who visited pulpits and opened her great heart to those who could use it. . . . Uncalled, unrobed, unanointed, she let her great heart beat in their presence. When warm weather came, Baby Suggs, holy, followed by every black man, woman and child who could make it through, took her great heart to the Clearing—a wide-open place cut deep in the woods nobody knew for what at the end of a path known only to deer and whoever cleared the land in the first place. In the heat of every Saturday afternoon, she sat in the clearing while the people waited among the trees.

After situating herself on a huge flat-sided rock, Baby Suggs bowed her head and prayed silently. The company watched her from the trees. They knew she was ready when she put her stick down. Then she shouted, "Let the children come!" and they ran from the trees towards her. "Let your mothers hear you laugh," she told them, and the woods rang. The adults looked on and could not help smiling. Then "Let the grown men come," she shouted. They stepped out one by one from among the ringing trees. "Let your wives and your children see you dance," she told them, and groundlife shuddered under their feet. Finally she called the women to her. "Cry," she told them. "For the living and the dead. Just cry." And without covering their eyes the women let loose. It started that way: laughing children, dancing men, crying women and then it got mixed up. Women stopped crying and danced; men sat down and cried; children danced, women laughed, children cried until, exhausted and riven, all and each lay about the Clearing damp and gasping for breath. In the silence that followed Baby Suggs, holy, offered up to them her great big heart. She did not tell them to clean up their lives or to go out and sin no more. She did not tell them they were the blessed of the earth, its inheriting meek or glorybound pure. She told them that the only grace they could have was the grace they could imagine. That if they could not see it, they would not have it.

Finding and nurturing intimacy is a gracious and imaginative endeavor, filling us with gladness of heart, and providing strength of spirit towards other hard work to be done, the unfinished business of seeking forgiveness.

Questions for pondering:

What intimacy do you want that you do not now enjoy, and what risks are you willing to take to seek it?

What relationships with family members and friends do you especially want to nurture now?

What intimate memories comfort and delight you?

What are your homing places? Your soul places?

※

6. Seeking Forgiveness

CORDELIA: For thee, oppressed king, am I cast
    down;
    Myself could else out-frown false fortune's
    frown.
    Shall we not see these daughters and these
    sisters?
LEAR: No, no, no, no! Come, let's away to prison:
    We two alone will sing like birds i' the cage:
    When thou dost ask me blessing, I'll kneel
    down
    And ask of thee forgiveness.
                              —William Shakespeare

At our age, the memory of rivalries and injuries of former years may seem no longer worth carrying. A longing grows to clear the decks of our primary relationships, to ask forgiveness of those one has wronged, so as to move into the elder season more lightly, at peace with the past. At the same time, if one has been deeply wounded or abused by another or others, one may be unable or unwilling to grant forgiveness, until some measure of justice, repentance, and healing has occurred. What does it mean to ask and to grant forgiveness on the elder journey? Who should take the initiative? In personal, social, and work relationships, how do we find ways to heal the past and move into the future with hope? Seeking forgiveness is the task to which we now turn.

The relationship of King Lear to his daughters provides a metaphor of forgiveness for our consideration.

Lear has three daughters: Regan and Goneril the two older, and the youngest, Cordelia. We deduce from the fact that all the "good" people in the play love him and all the "bad" people hate him, that he must have been a benevolent ruler for a long time. But he is also a proud and arrogant ruler and father, an excessively emotional man, unaware of his own capacity to make terrible mistakes or to do evil, or of the evil capabilities in others, especially those close to him. Unable to discern which of his daughters truly loves him, and over eighty years old, he decides to divest himself of his kingdom, and invites his daughters to affirm their love for him as a kind of test of which of them should get power and possessions. The two older daughters respond in flattering ways that please Lear. But they do not in fact love him. Cordelia, who truly loves her father, refuses to affirm her love in the false package required by Lear. Enraged by her recalcitrance, Lear, despite the protestations of his trusted counselor, Kent, disinherits and banishes her from his sight and kingdom, giving his power and authority over to the two elder daughters. They quickly move to strip him of even his modest retinue, reduce him to a state of humiliation, refusing even to provide him and his few followers hospitality in a great storm. Accompanied only by his court jester, Lear is exposed to the ravages of the storm and subject to physical and emotional deprivation such as he has never known. Maddened by the cruelty of his "monster daughters," his heart broken, Lear, undergoes a profound transformation. He begins to recognize his need of patience, and feels compassion for his court jester and others without power in his kingdom. He also begins to realize how badly he has misjudged his daughters. When he and Cordelia are thrown into prison, Lear comes to his senses, slowly recognizes Cordelia as his beloved daughter, and says to her, "You must bear with me. Pray you now, forget and forgive; I am old and foolish."

In this scene of the impending death of both father and daughter (though unknown to them), Cordelia asks her father about confronting "these daughters and these sisters." She is young and wants to fight, overcome, unmask these women. But Lear has, literally, no time for revenge, and no interest either. His buoyant, insistent "No, no, no, no!" signals a conversion of heart, a passion for living now, fully, joyously, even in prison. "Come, let's away to prison: / We too alone will sing like birds i' the cage." Lear is bent, not on revenge against daughters now lost to him, but on reconciliation with the daughter now found. Cordelia, throughout the play, is not only a human person, but a spirit, a symbol of Lear's inner child, the innocence, the true feeling that he has so brutally rejected, to which he so blessedly returns in these moments of rebirth. Lear becomes every inch a king, not in the time of his pomp and power, but in the time of his powerlessness. He is reborn into a second naïveté, a state of emancipated innocence, in which he is given a pure heart with eyes to see into the mystery of things.

The first order of business is asking Cordelia to

forgive him. "When thou dost ask me blessing, I'll kneel down / And ask of thee forgiveness." Lear's elegant gesture! When in social and familial protocol Cordelia, daughter and subject, prepares to kneel to ask Lear's blessing, he, preventing her, will kneel before her, father to daughter, king to subject, asking her forgiveness. He turns from fighting for his own kingdom to entering the kingdom of God through the portal of repentance and reconciliation. Author Helen Luke writes, "The blessing that the old may pass on to the young springs only out of that humility that is the fruit of wholeness, the humility that knows *how* to kneel, *how* to ask forgiveness."

Asking forgiveness of those whom we have wronged calls for the courage of humility.

Colleagues and Friends

Broken relationships with a colleague or friend weigh on us. I suffered such a breakage with a certain leader of Kirkridge workshops. A Jungian psychotherapist in his mid-sixties, he had done good work at Kirkridge for years and was well appreciated by participants. We developed a respecting, if not intimate, friendship. On one occasion, he led a workshop while sick, without his full energy. Participant response to the event was mixed. A Kirkridge staff person who coordinated the event wrote an evaluation, raising serious questions about the quality of the leadership. I wrote my colleague, sending the critique and inquiring about his "energy" to do this kind of work. I suggested that we enter into a dialogue about the matter and in the meantime reconsider a future date already agreed upon for his next workshop. He wrote back, expressing anger and frustration at what he felt was "betrayal" by both the Kirkridge staff person and me, and stated he was no longer available. We exchanged additional letters in which I expressed sadness at the rift between us, and he articulated continuing anger and disappointment at what he felt to be my presumptive judgment of his work.

A year went by. I remained saddened by this break, rare in my twenty years at Kirkridge. Perhaps in my youth or middle age I might have shrugged it off, figuring that "you can't win them all." But I was burdened by the thought of carrying this small sadness into retirement, and had come to feel that I had been substantially in the wrong in this matter. So I decided to try to make amends. I wrote my colleague,

Dear ———,

I found myself thinking of you a few days ago. So I re-read our correspondence of a year ago and have been pondering all that transpired between us. I conclude, in retrospect, that the way in which I raised concerns with you was unfair, ungracious, and presumptuous. I apologize. The personal break between us continues to sadden me. I hope we may find our way to some kind of reconciliation. Beyond this, I invite you to consider doing another workshop here. This letter brings my sincere and warm greetings to you. . . .

In ten days a letter came from him:

Dear Robert,

Glad to have your note of second thoughts re your responses to my leadership, or reported version thereof. That your responses I considered to be "unfair, ungracious, and presumptuous" pretty well covers it, so I'm happy to have you concur. That my responses were exaggerated and self-righteous and unnecessarily mean-spirited I would have to acknowledge, and apologize for them. Life is very short and precious, we both agree, so the less of these painful rifts the better for all concerned, and I too have been saddened about ours. So, yes, I trust these exchanges can free us both to go on with less baggage. . . . Warm greetings to you, then, and I'm happy that we are in touch, and thank you for the grace in you."

The details of how a relationship breaks are less important than the desire of both parties to heal it. Initiative may come from either side, but, to have hope of positive response, there must be some acknowledgment of wrongdoing where it exists, and apology. Therefore it is most hopeful if the one chiefly in the wrong takes the first step. It is always a risk to reach out. You may get a negative response or none at all, or, as in this case, a magnanimous one. Just as angry recrimination often begets anger, so, sometimes, admitting we were wrong and making apology begets generosity. At our age we may be willing to take such risks for the sake of a healing closure. In any case, upon the receipt of my colleague's letter I felt a glad relief and gratitude that we had come through a painful separation to a peaceful place.

Parents and Adult Children

Family strife is the most painful, and yields the greatest joy in reconciliation. Psychologist Sam Osherson tells of a thirty-nine-year-old man alienated from his father. The man told Osherson, "We had fought throughout my adolescence about who I dated, and which women were 'proper' for a person of my class and background. This was all during the 1960s, and his attitudes made me furious. So of course I started living with a woman completely unacceptable to him; she was never invited to the house." Unexpectedly, the father was hospitalized for his emphysema, and the son rushed to his bedside to find him on a respirator, close to death. "I walked in the room, and he smiled at me. He couldn't talk because of the tubes in his throat, but he wrote me a note. It said 'I want to meet Anne, I want everything to be . . .' And then he made a sign with his hands that meant 'A-OK . . . when I go.' I cried so when he did that, and we hugged. I said I wanted everything that way too. He died later that day, before he could meet her. But I can hardly tell you what those last words meant to me. It freed me from the guilt and anger I felt, it allowed me to realize how much he meant to me." The young man stopped and then added: "It meant I don't have to remember him being angry and disappointed in me. I think often of that final sign he made: let's leave everything A-OK."

The sign and note not only freed the son from guilt and anger, they also freed his father to die at peace with his son and at peace with himself. Most parents and their adult children want things to be "A-OK" between them and to work it all out before it's too late. There are some relationships beyond repair, like those of Lear and his two older daughters, others whose pattern of indifference or remoteness makes rapprochement unlikely, and some so fraught or bizarre as to be impossible. But sometimes when one party to an alienation reaches out, forgiveness is mutually discovered to be a swinging door waiting for a tiny push.

Birthdays may wake us up and offer an objective "excuse" to reach out, as was the case with me and my daughter Barb, as previously mentioned. Family occasions, such as anniversaries, graduations, weddings, or funerals, bring family members together in moments that may proffer unsolicited reconciliation in the celebration of family memory and hope. Of course things can turn sour on such occasions, and one or more family members may choose not to expose themselves to the potential pain of such an event. However, it is always possible that the desire to honor, remember, or succor one family member may allow resentments of the years to be set aside for the moment, and perhaps longer. And each time one makes it through such a family gathering with courtesy, there may be an easing of old antagonisms and a willingness to let healing take place, unspoken, but noticed. Often the family soul is generous and tough enough to contain specific separations without losing either party, retaining the context and possibility of future reconciliation.

Siblings

As mentioned earlier, I have noticed in recent years, in myself and each of my siblings, an increased desire to connect, to heal whatever wounds there may be, and to support one another in family sorrows and joys. My understanding of sibling relationships has been much enriched by Francine Klagsbrun's book *Mixed Feelings.* She mentions the research of Deborah Gold, who studies aging and developmental changes in later life and suggests that sibling relationships among older people can be classified into five types: intimate, congenial, loyal, apathetic, and hostile. Her classification is based on interviews with men and women over the age of sixty-five. Of course, as Klagsbrun states, "Many sibling relationships do not fall neatly into one of these five types." Her own research indicates that "relatively few place themselves in the most distant categories of apathy or hostility. Nor do the majority see themselves as 'very close,' intimate and unqualified best friends. Most people view themselves in the middle range of 'close' or 'somewhat close,' that place of mixed feelings, where warmth can sometimes slide into hostility, and resentment can be contained, when desired, by love and loyalty. . . . Siblings need to set their own thermostats, find their own comfort zones for involvement in one another's lives."

Our comfort zone with one sibling will probably differ from that with another. Each sibling relationship is of varying intensity or closeness. And as we age, we begin to understand that it is all right, and to be expected, that our relationships differ. It is not blamable to feel closer to or more at ease with one sibling rather than another, but simply a matter of fact, and perhaps also a matter of specific history, where we all fit into the chronology and pathology of our family experience.

My sister, Rose, is five years older than I. The friendly but unconnected relationship we shared in our patriarchal family of origin grew more remote down the years. During the period of my divorce and move to Pennsylvania, her two daughters got married, and I was so preoccupied with my own struggles I did not get to the weddings, a matter about which I still feel regret. I began to want my sister's comfort and understanding regarding my new life and new marriage, and I began to care about developing a significant connection with her. So I started making the effort to see her and her family whenever I could manage the trip. While at first she distrusted my motivations for this sudden renewed interest in our relationship, affection grew between us. The death of our parents in successive years, with the entire family gathering in her home for our own kind of wake, deepened our sense of common bond and nourished our family belonging. A few years later her son asked me to officiate at his wedding, and that occasion provided a delightful reunion. Now Rose and I see each other infrequently because of distance and illness. But we are closer, and it is because she has forgiven me for past neglect and indifference, and because I reached out to her, asking forgiveness, over these last many years. We both wanted reconciliation.

As we grow older, it is less lonely out there if those who have known us since childhood, and to whom we are bound by ties of blood and history, are adult friends. Or better still, if they are sisters and brothers we know we can count on to be there for us, and who know that we in turn can be similarly counted on, whatever happens. All of us know that more funerals lie ahead, as well as birthdays and anniversaries. Siblings are especially well positioned to help us keep on, as Emily Dickinson puts it, "sweeping up the heart" of our life.

The Dead

Some of us might wish to have the forgiveness of someone who has died. William Kennedy, in his novel *Ironweed*, tells the story of Francis Phelan, a minor-league baseball player in Albany. Francis accidentally dropped his thirteen-day-old baby boy while changing its diaper. The fall broke the baby's neck, and it died. Wild with grief, Francis later took part in a labor riot against management thugs in which he threw a rock at a man and killed him. Francis jumped on a train passing through town and became a fugitive, abandoning his family, joining "the brotherhood of the desolate." He lived the life of a hobo for twenty-two years. Then one year on All Saints' Day Francis was back in Albany. He found day labor as a gravedigger, and walked slowly up the hills of the cemetery where his dead parents and dead son, Gerald,

lay waiting for him. As he came among the tomb-
stones, his father, Michael Phelan

was already following the line of his son's walk
towards the plot beneath the box elder tree where
Gerald was buried. . . . Francis had never seen
Gerald's grave . . . had not attended Gerald's
funeral. His absence that day was the scandal of the
resident population of St. Agnes. . . . But here he
was now, walking purposefully . . . closing the gap
between father and son, between sudden death
and enduring guilt. . . . Michael signaled to his
neighbors that an act of regeneration seemed to be
in process, and the eyes of the dead, witnesses to
all their own historical omissions, their own
unbridgeable chasm in life gone, silently rooted for
Francis. . . . In his grave . . . Gerald watched the
advent of his father and considered what action
might be appropriate to their meeting. . . . Should
he absolve the man of all guilt, not for the dropping, for that was accidental, but for the abandonment of the family. . . ? Gerald's grave trembled
with superb possibility. . . . Francis found the
grave without a search. He stood over it and
reconstructed the moment when the child was
slipping through his fingers into death. He prayed
for a repeal of time so that he might hang himself
in the coal bin before picking up the child to
change its diaper. Denied that, he prayed for his
son's eternal peace in the grave. . . . Tears oozed
from Francis' eyes, and when one of them fell
onto his shoetop, he pitched forward onto the
grave, clutching the grass, remembering the diaper

in his grip. "I remember everything," Francis told Gerald in the grave. "It's the first time I tried to think of these things since you died. . . . Your mother said two words, 'Sweet Jesus,' and then we both crouched down to snatch you up. But we both stopped in that crouch because of the look of you. . . . [I hear] your mother never blamed me for dropping you. Never told a soul in 22 years it was me let you fall. Is that some woman or isn't it? I remember the linoleum you fell on was yellow with red squares. You suppose now that I can remember this stuff out in the open, I can finally start to forget it?

Francis, lost for twenty-two years, found his own way to kneel before his lost son and ask forgiveness. Unable to forgive himself or forget the terrible day, Francis made pilgrimage to the holy place of harrowing and healing. Whatever else the doctrine of the Communion of the Saints means, it invites us to gather in the company of those who have died and to seek reconciliation that eluded us in life. We may hope that the dead are rooting for us and that healing of our history may yet be granted. Deep in our hearts, we know, we all know, that only a general and complete amnesty will clear out our souls and forgive our sins. We know that we must begin with the most heinous, grief-laden choices, accidents, mistakes, and betrayals of our lives, bringing (in Francis Phelan's phrase) "this stuff out in the open" to learn whether we will be forgiven, and whether we can now forgive ourselves after all these years. For some of us, forgiving ourselves is the hardest part.

The Nation

In 1995, in his seventy-ninth year, Robert McNamara published his book *In Retrospect: The Tragedy and Lessons of Vietnam*, offering the public "a glimpse of his aching conscience. The most willful Vietnam warrior in the Kennedy and Johnson administrations, he was also the first at the top to admit defeat, in private. He then stood silent on the war for a quarter-century and drowned his sorrow in good works at the World Bank." So wrote Max Frankel in his *New York Times* review of the book. Why did McNamara go public now? He writes about policies he initially championed and then argued against privately to President Johnson, policies that resulted in the deaths of some sixty thousand Americans and hundreds of thousands of Vietnamese, and hundreds of thousands more wounded, not to mention severe damage to the American economy, and the nation's tortured legacy of the Vietnam War. McNamara acknowledges, "What we did was terribly, terribly wrong." The book is an anguished mea culpa from a man asking forgiveness of the American people. The *New York Times* editorial on the book, "Mr. McNamara's War," insists that he "must not escape the lasting moral condemnation of his countrymen." Others pointed out, in theologian Robert McAfee Brown's words, that it is "a great and almost unprecedented moral achievement for a man in public life to have offered such an honest accounting of how people like himself, with initially good intentions, became enmeshed in structures of their own creation from which it was finally impossible to escape."

While no one can forgive on behalf of other people, especially the dead, one can honor McNamara's remorse, respect his courage to admit terrible mistakes, and perhaps feel some sympathy for one who still cannot forgive himself after all these years. For all of us, the only way towards the possibility of forgiveness is in making the pilgrimage of confession, risking whatever condemnation or understanding may await from peers, ourselves, and God. Such "kneeling" grace penetrates distance, time, death, and all other barriers. If time and death cannot be repealed, there may be healing in a heavenly overwrite, whether the healing is in our souls alone, in relationships accessible to present reconciliation, or in the underground river of eternity.

Personal Enemies

But what about those who have wounded *us*, are not penitent or asking forgiveness, simply don't care, are unavailable for engagement, or are dead? It's one thing to *ask* forgiveness of those who have wronged us. It's quite another to *grant* forgiveness to those who have abused, betrayed, or oppressed us—even considering that the granting of forgiveness calls for the courage of hope. But how does one whose heart is still filled with rage, hurt, and even hatred have any room for hope?

Thank God for the Psalms. There are those who regard the Psalms as spiritually inferior literature because some of them are filled with anger and hatred, and are so "bloodthirsty." One would have to grant, however, that they are real prayers of real people

struggling for help and hope, beseeching and besieg-
ing God to redress grievances. They are honest prayers that have not been sanitized for liturgical or
theological reasons. They are not "spiritually correct"
prayers, and therefore, sometimes, some of them may
be *our* prayers.

Hebrew scripture scholar Walter Brueggemann
points out that over half the Psalms deal with enemies
and the psalmist's desire for revenge. He says: "Those of
us who find some dimension of vengeance in our bodies
can't love our enemies until we give our vengeance to
God; Psalms of vengeance are cries from underneath,
appeals to God against the rulers, jailors, betrayers,
oppressors of his age. . . . These prayers are almost dys-
functional for us because we don't have a strong enough
God." That is, unlike Job and Jesus, who accused God
of injustice and abandonment respectively, we often
don't think God can handle the full load of our anguish
and anger. The speaker in Psalm 109, a person who has
suffered massive betrayal, a theft of property or reputation by a supposed friend, *did* think God could handle it
all. Here is part of the prayer, telling us what the speaker
wants God to do to his enemy:

> Appoint a wicked man [read "hanging judge"]
>   against him;
>   let an accuser bring him to trial.
> When he is tried, let him come forth guilty;
>   let his prayer be counted as sin!
> May his days be few;
>   may another seize his goods!
> May his children be fatherless,
>   and his wife a widow!

May his children wander about and beg;
    may they be driven out of the ruins they inhabit!
May the creditor seize all that he has;
    may strangers plunder the fruits of his toil!
Let there be none to extend kindness to him,
    nor any to pity his fatherless children!
May his posterity be cut off;
    may his name be blotted out in the second
        generation!
May the iniquity of his fathers be remembered
        before the Lord,
    And let not the sin of his mother be blotted out!

This psalmist has earnestly tried to remember every possible calamity that could befall the enemy so as to commend it to God. He or she is an enthusiastic hater and vengeance-seeker, in brief, saying to God, "This jackass didn't stand in solidarity with me in my need, and I propose nobody stand with him in his need." Is there any reader who does not feel that his or her rage and lust for vengeance is not adequately represented here?

Whose prayer might this be today?

Could it be the prayer of a Bosnian Muslim woman raped by a Christian Bosnian Serb soldier as part of the policy of ethnic cleansing? Or, perhaps, the prayer of that woman's husband or parents? Might it be the prayer of a Holocaust survivor, the prayer of a parent whose child was murdered, the prayer of a farmer who lost the family farm to the bank after six generations, the prayer of one sabotaged by a friend or betrayed by a lover? Is it your prayer? Has it ever been your prayer?

Ralph, a seventy-three-year-old friend, wrote: "I've denied anger as un-Christian and turned it inward. So I was shaken by being sued by our ex-son-in-law on the very day our daughter died (they had been divorced for seven years), to 'get his girls' as natural father. My anger flared and has continued as we fight it out in court. We've won temporarily, and have custody, but how do we forgive him? How do we get our feelings out when we are not to write or speak to him (except for visitation arrangements)? We have written letters of anger and filed them. We have shared the hurt with our family and friends. I have dreamed about it and imagined conversation. I have asked when I might ask forgiveness for myself and tell him how he hurt me. The answer I heard was: not until it is mutual. He would only be defensive if he doesn't see it our way. What does it mean to return good for evil here, and to love your enemies? I must work on this one." Hats off to Ralph, who *is* "working on this one," as you and I must with our own complicated issues and relationships of forgiveness.

As we work our way through Psalm 109, acknowledging and owning our thirst for vengeance, and our inability to get justice or even apology, we finally come to verse 21:

> But thou, O God my Lord, deal on my behalf
>   for thy name's sake;
>   because thy steadfast love is good, deliver me!

We turn our vengeance over to God, taking no destructive action ourselves, but putting it on God's desk, remembering that God is a God of justice: "Vengeance is mine, I will repay, says the Lord." God is not appalled at our hatred and outrage. God is strong enough to handle our assault. We can take it *all* to the Lord in prayer. In other words, we don't have to check our violent passions at the door of prayer. As we exhaust every means to engage the oppressor or betrayer in a dialogue of grievance, apology, and restitution, we can offer ourselves and that person up to God, and let the vengeance energy about what cannot be changed drain away, allowing a measure of relief to flow into the heart. When our hit list and our prayer list begin to overlap, it is possible the Holy One is getting to us, and we may be able to let go of the bitter burden of what can never be forgiven.

National Enemies

But how does one grant forgiveness to the bureaucrats of evil in political and economic systems that oppress? During the fiftieth anniversaries of VE and VJ Days ending World War II and of the dropping of the first atomic bombs on Hiroshima and Nagasaki, we Americans continued to debate in 1995 who should apologize to whom about wartime atrocities. While the German nation apologized years ago, the Japanese hadn't until August 1995, when Prime Minister Tomiichi Murayama used the word *owabi*, an unambiguous word for apology, referring explicitly to Japan's brutalities during the period of their "colonial rule" and "invasion." These included massacre of civilian populations, sexual enslavement, forced labor, and gruesome experiments on Chinese and other

Asians. But Americans are deeply divided over the question of apologizing to the Japanese people for dropping the first two nuclear bombs, not on military targets, but on the population centers of those cities.

Forgiving the past requires joining with those whom we regarded as complicit with evil policies, whether in our own country or others, to shape a human future, while not precluding the necessity of war crimes trials, when justified, in order to yield some measure of justice to victims and oppressors, and to set the record straight.

Theologian Carter Heyward led a seminary team participating in the insurrection against the brutal Somoza regime in Nicaragua. The team wrote a book called *Revolutionary Forgiveness* relating their experiences. One team member wrote: "I learned in Nicaragua that forgiveness is a revolutionary virtue. It is revolutionary not because everyone is forgiven or because forgiveness is all in God's hands. . . . Forgiveness is revolutionary because the former victims of an unjust system—such as that of Somoza—are able to see the systemic character of victimization and recognize thereby their former oppressors also as victims. Those who forgive are prepared to blame the way society was structured rather than simply the individuals who participated in it. The individuals are held responsible primarily for the future, not the past. They are given a chance to change rather than being cast away."

When Yitzhak Rabin and Yasir Arafat made their famous handshake on either side of President Clinton in 1993, it was an act of revolutionary forgiveness, having nothing to do with personal reconciliation and everything to do with the hope of mutual survival in the future. As Rabin said, "You don't make peace with friends but enemies." Revolutionary forgiveness is a hard-nosed bet on the future, a bet that you could lose. It calls for the courage of hope. And it makes space for hope to do its healing work.

The mystery of the disarmed heart is deeper than militarist or pacifist ideologies or strategies. It has to do with personal transformation of the sort that happened to Lear. It is rare at any age, and in any era, though perhaps elders are more vulnerable to such grace than the young. We have seen a remarkable example of it in the black people of South Africa. Mildred Motsuenane, a blind, arthritic mother of ten children, was weeping in triumph after voting for the first time in her life in a church in the Soweto ghetto on April 29, 1994. "I can tell you dawn is breaking and the dark night is gone. My parents never saw this day. My husband never saw this day. Now I'm going to the cemetery and tell his bones that I voted."

What great joy it was watching those throngs weaving their patient way to vote, watching Nelson Mandela, amazingly free of bitterness, join hands with Prime Minister F. W. de Klerk, taking the path of revolutionary forgiveness, welcoming all, oppressed and oppressors, into the new country. It was so beautiful because we feared it would never happen, surely not in our lifetime. It was like the reign of God happening before our very eyes. It *was* the reign of God happening, because human liberation is always the sign of God's activity in history and in our lives.

Two years later President Mandela made a state visit to London. Journalist Youssef Ibrahim described

his four-day triumphal sweep as "like a coronation."
He writes:

> From Buckingham Palace, where he stayed as
> the honored guest of the Queen, to the festively
> decorated streets of Brixton, home to one of
> Britain's largest black communities, Mr. Mandela
> was feted as a king in a country where Margaret
> Thatcher once called him a "terrorist" and dismissed
> the possibility that he could one day govern South
> Africa as a pipe dream out of "cloud-cuckoo land."
> . . . Addressing a joint meeting of Parliament at
> Westminster Hall on Thursday [July 11, 1996] . . .
> President Mandela . . . limped to the rostrum hold-
> ing the hand of the strong-minded Laborite Speaker
> of the House of Commons, Betty Boothroyd, who
> introduced him by saying, "You spent more than a
> third of your life in prison, though your spirit was
> freer there than those of your captors outside." . . .
> Reminding all that the African National Congress,
> which he led for many years while in jail, had come
> to Britain to seek justice and had been turned away,
> . . . he went on to make clear that while he has
> forgiven he has not forgotten. . . . This morning
> he carried the forgiving further, inviting Lady
> Thatcher—who as prime minister in the 1980s
> refused to endorse international sanctions against the
> white supremacist government—to Buckingham
> Palace, where they held a 20-minute chat. No
> details were released, but when earlier in the week
> he was asked about her stand, Mr. Mandela said,
> "Let bygones be bygones." She said nothing.

The possibility of revolutionary forgiveness sometime in the future does not cut the nerve of resistance against present evil and the current struggle for social justice. While Jesus encouraged people to forgive one another seventy times seven, and to pray: Forgive us our trespasses *as* we forgive those who trespass against us—he wasn't always able to manage it himself. While he could handle hatred and vilification directed at himself, he was often filled with outrage at the cruelty done to others, broke sacred Sabbath laws that prevented the healing of the sick, and even did property damage in the Temple to dramatize the human damage being perpetrated by the Temple system. Yet among his final words was the prayer "Father, forgive them, for they know not what they do."

Sometimes, without warning, in the least likely place, a strange grace subverts vengeance, and compassion overwhelms enmity. In 1944, when Yevgeny Yevtushenko, one of Russia's most loved poets, was nine years old, his mother took him from Siberia to Moscow. They were among those who witnessed a procession of twenty thousand German war prisoners being marched through the streets of Moscow. He writes,

> The pavements swarmed with onlookers, cordoned off by soldiers and police. The crowd was mostly women—Russian women with hands roughened by hard work, lips untouched by lipstick, and with thin hunched shoulders which had borne half of the burden of the war. Every one of them must have had a father or a husband, a brother or a son killed by the Germans. They

gazed with hatred in the direction from which the column was to appear.

At last we saw it. The generals marched at the head, massive chins stuck out, lips folded disdainfully, their whole demeanour meant to show superiority over their plebian victors. "They smell of perfume, the bastards," someone in the crowd said with hatred. The women were clenching their fists. The soldiers and policemen had all they could do to hold them back.

All at once something happened to them. They saw German soldiers, thin, unshaven, wearing dirty, blood-stained bandages, hobbling on crutches or leaning on the shoulders of their comrades; the soldiers walked with their heads down. The street became dead silent—the only sound was the shuffling of boots and the thumping of crutches.

Then I saw an elderly women in broken-down boots push herself forward and touch a policeman's shoulder, saying, "Let me through." There must have been something about her that made him step aside. She went up to the column, took from inside her coat something wrapped in a coloured handkerchief and unfolded it. It was a crust of black bread. She pushed it awkwardly into the pocket of a soldier, so exhausted that he was tottering on his feet. And now from every side women were running towards the soldiers, pushing into their hands bread, cigarettes, whatever they had. The soldiers were no longer enemies. They were people.

When sheer grace opens the eyes of our hearts to see enemies as people, compassion leads the way to forgiveness. Theologian Reinhold Niebuhr wrote: "Nothing worth doing is completed in our lifetime; therefore, we must be saved by hope. Nothing true or beautiful or good makes complete sense in any immediate context of history; therefore, we must be saved by faith. Nothing we do, however virtuous, can be accompanied alone; therefore we are saved by love. No act is quite as virtuous from the standpoint of our friend or foe as from our own standpoint. Therefore, we must be saved by the final form of love which is forgiveness."

Forgiveness allows us to heal or accept the past, letting it be, letting it go, and opens a way for us to walk into the future, exploring the abiding mystery of life and death.

Questions for pondering:

Whom do you need to ask for forgiveness?

Whom are you ready to consider forgiving?

Where might the bitterness be drained from your soul?

Might you seek a general amnesty from God for an unhealed relationship with someone who has died?

7· Taking On the Mystery

LEAR: . . . so we'll live,
   And pray, and sing, and tell old tales and laugh
   At gilded butterflies, and hear poor rogues
   Talk of court news; and we'll talk with them
      too.
   Who loses and who wins; who's in, who's out;
   And take upon's the mystery of things,
   As if we were God's spies.
                          —William Shakespeare

At a workshop on spiritual eldering, led by theologian and author Zalman Schachter-Shalomi, participants were asked to estimate how many years they had left to live: based on age, health, and parental longevity. We ranged in age from fifty-five to seventy-eight and estimated our years left to live from six to over thirty. We were then invited to make up a menu for the rest of our lives, considering the following: What do I have appetite for? What do I want to taste again and again, or for the first time? What do I not want to stomach any longer? What, for me, would be a healthy diet for living? We were encouraged not to censor our wants or try to make them politically or theologically correct.

Here are some samplings from our menus:

I want to sing more. There is a Hindu saying that God respects me when I work, but God loves me when I sing.

I want to visit sacred places, to complete my master's program, to visit the moon, to mentor younger men, to be more playful and prayerful.

I want time for woodworking and to have a vegetable garden. I want to go to Scandinavia, to live for a year in a Third World country, and to work for a year as a church or school custodian. I want to spend time at the ocean and read the lives of our country's presidents.

I want to want. There's no passion in me. I'm ready to die or be reborn.

I want to get to know more of my unconscious. I want to become intimately familiar with a plot of wilderness in all four seasons. I want to ski more: the only time I feel graceful is when I'm skiing. I want more time alone.

I want a continuing sense of outrage about the injustices in our country; I don't want to live an epicurean life.

I want to practice nonattachment with my children, learn to play a musical instrument, eat a hot fudge sundae without getting heartburn.

I want more intimacy with nature and people. I feel my sexuality coming alive again. I want to learn to partner another, and I want lots of laughter in my life.

I want my own place. I want the relationship with my daughter to heal. I want work that fills me instead of empties me. I want to learn to be able to ask for help.

I found the exercise personally evocative. My own estimate is that, with luck, I may have fifteen years left to live. And my menu for those years? I want mornings by myself, for reading, study, writing. I want more invitations to speak and to conduct workshops than I will choose to accept, and I hope to write a few more books. I want a daily walk along our country road, two, three miles by the farms and along the lake, and back. I want evenings with my wife, for dining and talk, and just being together. I want to enjoy my children, grandchildren, and siblings and their families, with frequent visits, tasting as deeply as I can the unique beauty of each life, and lending support in the ways available to me, and accepting the comfort of their care when I need it. I want to savor old friendships and develop new ones. I want energy. Having lived most of my life in a parsonage, I want years of enjoying our modest but lovely home and tasting the pleasure of owning a small piece of land. I want to participate in a spiritually vibrant and socially active congregation, working through church and community agencies for a greater degree of racial, sexual, and economic justice in our region and nation. I want to take courses in poetry. I want more music and drama in my life. I would enjoy an occasional winter visit to northern California to see the coastal mountains and watch the migrating gray whales. I want to live more deeply into the mystery of my self and creation.

One does not look for much originality in such choices, for we are on a common journey, though eccentricity is to be cherished by ourselves if not others, and every singular delight savored. I note that many of my choices are available to me now, that most don't require additional resources, and that my youthful desire to "change the world" has distilled into the hope of living into my own integrity and helping to heal my small corner of creation.

So, how many years might you have left to live?

What's on your menu?

. . . so we'll live

The first item on Lear's menu is asking forgiveness of his daughter Cordelia. But then he soars into a doxology of the human vocation which gives wings to our own hopes.

Whether we have ten days or ten years or thirty years, now, here, in this moment, we are learning that life is precious. We no longer want to kill time but to savor it, taste each moment, notice some of the things we missed hurrying through former years. Imprisoned and about to be executed, Lear had only moments to live. Whatever the context of our confinement or limitation of body, relationship, or circumstance, whatever the shape of our lost opportunities and hedged hopes, we want to live fully every day, as sensuously, as awake and alive as possible.

As I write these words this morning, I hear the rain outside falling softly on the leaves of the trees and gently pattering on the roof of the sunroom. Finishing my morning writing, I do the laundry, feed our dog, and make spaghetti to take later this afternoon to a woman of our congregation who is dying of AIDS. There are errands to do. A "normal" day, but *my* day to live quietly and passionately, with the eyes and ears of my heart open. Like my friend Jerry.

Jerry is in his sixties and lives in Washington, D.C. Because of certain disabilities, he spends a good deal of time in his apartment and has learned to observe people living their lives on the streets outside his window. He described "an elderly woman I often saw from my apartment window, shuffling up the street, bent almost double, carrying her shopping bag as she went to and from the grocery. In each direction, she had to cross the five traffic lanes of busy 16th Street. She did it at the light, of course, but traffic engineers, it seems to me, are in the business of moving vehicles and holding down the population, and so she never could get across during the time the light was red for the flow. Drivers had to have mercy, which they did. She looked as if she could have used a lot of help in living, but perhaps she was a woman of resolution and independence, possible subject for a new kind of profile in courage. I have not seen her for a year or more."

Jerry watched that old woman walk day by day, and because he *saw* her, her small daily acts of courage evoked his compassion and admiration. Because he *saw* her, she became a frequent presence in his life, and when she was no longer there on the street, he missed her. She ennobled his humanity, and now we too are touched by her dogged living day by day, and wonder what has happened to her. Jerry has a good eye, and reminds us how much there is to see out there if the eyes of our hearts are open.

When we are caught up in the routine of our daily life, going through the motions but not savoring the moment, a sudden loss or illness may wake us up, or a reprieve from danger or pain may open the eyes of our hearts. In Alexander Solzhenitsyn's novel *Cancer Ward*, Oleg has suffered months with his cancer, and seems to be surviving it. The day for his release from the hospital arrives:

Early in the morning . . . Oleg got up quietly. . . . It was the morning of creation. The world had been created anew for one reason only, to be given back to Oleg. "Go out and live!" it seemed to say. . . . His face radiated happiness . . . with that early-morning springtime joy that touches even the old and sick. . . . The first morning of creation . . . [Oleg] conceived the mad scheme of going to the Old Town immediately, while it was still early morning, to look at a flowering apricot tree. He walked through the forbidden gates, [got on a trolley to the Old Town, and looked at people on the trolley as though they were the first human beings he had ever seen. He got off, walked down a side street, stopped at a teahouse, sat down and began to sip his tea]. And then from the teahouse balcony he saw above the walled courtyard next door something pink and transparent. It looked like a puff dandelion, only it was six meters in diameter, a rosy, weightless balloon. He'd never seen anything so pink and so huge. . . . He walked up to the railings and from on high gazed through this pink miracle. It was his present to himself—his creation-day present. It was like a

fire tree decorated with candles. . . . The flowering apricot was the only tree in the courtyard
. . . open to the sky . . . Oleg examined it—pink-
ness, that was the general impression. The tree had
buds like candles. When on the point of opening,
the petals were pink in color, but once open they
were pure white, like apple or cherry blossoms.
The result was an incredible, tender pink. Oleg
was trying to absorb it all into his eyes. He wanted
to remember it for a long time. . . . He'd planned
on finding a miracle, and he had found one.

When one really wakes up, every day is the first
morning of creation. We never know when we might
find a miracle, and all we want to do is *live* that
day with all five senses on alert, for (in Yeats's
words) "twenty minutes more or less," so great is our
happiness.

. . . so we'll live,
And pray . . .

Prayer is as natural as breathing; it is the soul doing
what comes naturally. To pray is to allow our deepest
yearnings to pour out in hope and despair, to cry out
in rage against injustice, to praise the source of all
beauty and love. As Rilke writes, praising is what matters, and the more the soul praises, the stronger it
grows. We may or may not use language addressed to
God or offer our deepest concerns to the source of all
being, but whenever we pour out our heart, we are
praying. Prayers of the heart need no religious language nor any words at all. The apostle Paul reminds
us that we do not know how to pray as we ought but

the Spirit helps us in our weakness, searching our hearts with sighs too deep for words (Romans 8:26ff). I used to sigh a lot, before my tears could get wet on my cheeks. What a comfort to know that our sighs, the deepest yearnings of our soul, are already our response to the Spirit searching our heart. God is the unceasing intercessor, and our praying participates in the ongoing yearning from the heart of the universe for the healing and liberation of all creation.

Theologian John Biersdorf writes, "The description of the holographic or implicate order [in modern physics] is stunningly reminiscent of the territory in which the mystics experience the divine presence. The holographic domain seems alike to be the depth of knowing of which humans are capable, the fundamental nature of reality, and the arena for profound prayer." When we pray we are conspiring with God towards the healing of creation, going deep into the well of our own souls in a work of "unconsciousness raising." Dialoguing with our unconscious means becoming spelunkers, specialists of the inward journey, searching out the depths of our own cavernous histories. Rinzai Zen Buddhism suggests that there are three requirements for such rigorous practice: "A great root of faith, a great ball of doubt, and a great tenacity of purpose."

Theologian Abraham Heschel writes: "To pray is to pull ourselves together, to pour our perception, volition, memory, thought, hope, feeling, dreams, all that is moving in us into one tone. Not the words we utter, the service of the lips, but the way in which the devotion of the heart corresponds to what the words contain . . . is the pith of prayer." We hand over our time to God, says Heschel, in the secrecy of single words. So, for me, prayer comes down to such words as *bless*, *thank you*, *help*, *forgive*, *open*, *heal*. In the face of brutal and tragic realities in the world or in our own personal scene, praying is a refusal to stop hoping for what we passionately want or need for ourselves or those we love or care about in the world. It isn't a matter of the odds for such healing or reconciliation or liberation. It is simply a matter of asking, seeking, knocking on the doors of hope. It isn't a matter of specific outcomes so much as the experience of the psalmist: "On the day I called, You answered me. You increased my strength of soul" (Psalm 138:3).

Vaclav Havel, former president of Czechoslovakia, put it this way: "Hope is an orientation of the heart. . . . The more unpropitious the situation in which we demonstrate hope, the deeper that hope is. . . . [Without hope] it is impossible to live in dignity and meaning much less find the will for the 'hopeless enterprise' which stands at the beginning of most good things." Havel lived long enough to see the hopeless enterprise of freedom in Europe become a reality, though a bloody, ethnically contentious one whose future remains uncertain.

How could we who, in a few short years, have seen the tearing down of the Berlin Wall, the end of apartheid and the election of Mandela in South Africa, the tortured but still alive peace process between Israel and the Palestinians, and the peace negotiations in northern Ireland not keep on hoping in all circumstances, great and small? I like the words of New Testament scholar Walter Wink: "History belongs to the intercessors who believe the future into being." Though our efforts fail and our hopes be disappointed again and again, nothing in all creation can stop the tide of judgment. No dikes can forever withstand the rolling waters of justice or defend against the healing river. Time, space, death wash away like sand. All that is, was, or ever will be is porous with praying. Confinement, whatever the limitations of our circumstances, is no barrier to prayer, as Lear knew. On the contrary, prison cells, hospital rooms, subway trains, offices, kitchens, assembly lines, rocking chairs, lonely apartments provide occasion for prayers from the heart, sighs and songs too deep for words. We may find in our later years a newborn innocence about prayer and a fresh desire to pray in our own way day by day.

One may have learned to pray or taught someone to pray quite unwittingly. Educator Herrymon Maurer in a pamphlet titled *Simple Prayer* describes the praying of his grandmother:

Nothing is as secret as prayer and nothing more social. At the age of five, I lived for a time with my grandmother and came to learn of her . . . practice of retiring to her room sometime during the afternoon and sitting with her eyes closed in a rocking-chair which she did not rock. . . . From time to time she would utter the words, "O God!" Although spoken quietly, the words were not really spoken at all, but drawn forth in a tone that was joyful beyond joy and sorrowful beyond sorrow, a tone so unlike any pronouncements heard in church that the possibility of their being prayer did not consciously occur to me. . . . I came to learn slowly, since I was not told and did not imagine myself asking, that what went on in the rocking-chair was some sort of intensification of what went on in the rest of her life, and that this intensification was, in fact, prayer. What is prayer but the secret holding-up of all life to the light of truth?

Nowadays, I try to pray as my grandmother prayed. I know it is she I imitate, not because we talked about praying (it was not once discussed), but because the event remembered from childhood helped draw me toward simple prayer . . . of the sort that unites with all others who pray in the secret manner. Such prayer is not a matter for experts. In such a matter there can be no expertise, no display of intellect, no edifice of logic, no construction of theology, nor any other aspect of the exclusiveness that leads men and women to complex explanations of the universe and, too often, to quarrels with other explainers. In private prayer, there can be only ourselves, our neighbors, and the one God who is of all faiths and who is certainly not ours alone. As soon as I came to understand that my grandmother was praying, I understood also that she was praying not about herself but about everything that happened and everyone she met. Very simply and very secretly she held everything and everyone up to God. . . . Even as a child I sensed that she was an uplifting person simply because she constantly lifted things up.

If much of our praying consists of lifting things up to God, there are also seasons of what can be called "letting go and letting God" prayer. In a sermon entitled "Sinking Eternally into God," Meister Eckhart wrote, "We should sink eternally from something into nothing. . . . Let your 'being you' sink and flow into God's 'being God.' " Sinking into God, then, is letting go of control, security of place, or identity, letting go all our images, definitions, projections of the Holy One. But we're afraid of sinking. "Sink or swim" expresses our fear of drowning, being overwhelmed by despair, accident, or the power of others. Sinking seems to us a way into total vulnerability, a way of losing autonomy, a way into death. Our fear of sinking may be, most deeply, fear of the holy, of intimacy, of being taken over by Another, fear of risking and possibly losing the self in the ambiguous embrace of the unknown.

Sinking into God is falling into sleep, floating into that darkness which is like the darkness of death, going down into that dreamworld which terrifies and delights us, watching in the shadows for the Dreamer.

Sinking into God is spiraling down into our inner deeps, which are the deeps of the holoverse, going down, down, down into a place of silence.

Sinking into God is yielding to the tears that come and come and keep on coming, the pouring out of our sorrow and the pain of humanity and the groaning of creation and the love of God—rolling through us, cleansing our souls, caressing our bodies, quieting our minds, healing our hearts.

Sinking into God is undergoing the finitude of our

years, hallowing our diminishments, and accepting
the solitude of our being.
Sinking into God is slipping into the undertow of
God's severe grace, letting go all our betrayals, and
being swept out on waves of tender mercy.
Sinking into God is confiding all souls to the One
who tenders our souls.
Sinking into God is falling into the mystery which
names us and claims us.

. . . so we'll live,
And pray, and sing . . .

Sing like birds in the cage, singing their hearts out,
oblivious of their captivity. Our singing is not dependent on external freedom but comes from the heart.
The psalmist's question "How shall we sing the Lord's
song in a foreign land?" is answered by another posed
in the hymn "How Can I Keep from Singing?"

The essence of soul is to sing. The song of the
soul transcends limitations of the flesh, filling the canvas
of creation with the vast panoply of human art. Soul
sings in architecture, dance, painting, sculpture, music,
literature. My soul sings especially in reading—of
poetry, novels, biographies, histories, and books of
many other fields. One of the things for which I am
most grateful to my parents is the love of reading they
encouraged in me. That and the quality of schooling
they offered me, gave me a lifelong love of reading and
learning. When Margaret Truman Daniel, daughter of
President Harry S. Truman, was asked what her father's
image of heaven might be, she responded, "a good
comfortable chair, a good reading lamp, and lots of
books around that he wanted to read."

Last fall, in the first months of my retirement, a fantasy was fulfilled. I had hoped, in retirement, to study Shakespeare with a master teacher. Shortly after we moved to Connecticut, I got the Yale bulletin of courses for that school year. I noticed a course titled "Shakespeare and Originality," a seminar taught by Harold Bloom, a world-class humanities scholar. I just showed up in that seminar one day and after class introduced myself and asked Mr. Bloom for the privilege of auditing, and he graciously agreed. So I studied Shakespeare's plays and poetry week by week, from October to April, and every Wednesday afternoon from 1:30 to 3:30 attended the seminar, luxuriating in the commentary and rich insights of the teacher. What a treat! I hadn't studied Shakespeare since college days, nearly fifty years before. What did I know then? What I know now is that I want to read and learn and study under great teaching as long as I am able to do so. To paraphrase Walt Whitman, "I hear humanity singing, the varied carols I hear," modern and ancient songs of the soul.

In 1995 cave paintings twenty thousand years old were discovered in France. There were over three hundred Stone Age murals in red hematite, ochre yellow, and hues of charcoal. The team of explorers saw hordes of beasts in the beam of their flashlights: lions running, a group of horses' heads, cave bears with their mouths open, a pair of rhinoceroses fighting. Jean Clottes, France's foremost rock art specialist, said that after the first hour of scrutinizing the art and slowly accepting its authenticity, he paused. "I stood in front of that exquisite panel with the four horses' heads and I felt I was watching the work of a great master. I was so overcome that I cried. It was like going into an attic and finding a da Vinci. Except that this great master was unknown." And an ancestor from twenty thousand years ago.

Museums give us moments of communion with artists and their subjects of long ago, and sometimes we may be overcome with the immense journey humanity has taken and the mystery of our own participation in its beauty and sorrow. At the Holocaust Museum in Washington, D.C., staff have their favorite overheard comments of museumgoers. One was the comment of a young African-American male to another: "You see, I told you it wasn't just us."

I hear nature singing, the varied carols I hear. Nature presents a vast choir of song. St. Francis reminds us that all creatures sing their songs of praise in the great canticle of creation, raising their alleluias to the Creator. Diane Ackerman, in *A Natural History of the Senses*, tells of whales crooning in the depths of the sea: "Lone, inactive males start to sing during winter, the breeding season, and continue their ballads until company arrives to interrupt them. Their songs often last fifteen minutes or so, and they repeat like carols over many hours." Songbirds waken us at dawn with their early arias, while darkness falls upon the lonely lament of the loon. Our souls sing along with the unending chorus of praise.

One day anthropologist Loren Eiseley leaned against a stump at the edge of a small glade and fell asleep:

> When I awoke, dimly aware of some commotion and outcry in the clearing, the light was slanting

down through the pines in such a way that the glade was lit like some vast cathedral. I could see the dust motes of wood pollen in the long shaft of light, and there on the extended branch sat an enormous raven with a red and squirming nestling in his beak. The sound that awoke me was the outraged cries of the nestling's parents, who flew helplessly in circles about the clearing. The sleek black monster was indifferent to them. He gulped, whetted his beak on the dead branch a moment and sat still. Up to that point the little tragedy had followed the usual pattern. But suddenly, out of all that area of woodland, a soft sound of complaint began to rise. Into the glade fluttered small birds of half a dozen varieties drawn by the anguished outcries of the tiny parents. No one dared to attack the raven. But they cried there in some instinctive common misery. The bereaved and the unbereaved. . . . The sighing died. It was then I saw the judgment. It was the judgment of life against death. I will never see it again so forcefully presented. I will never hear it again in notes so tragically prolonged. For in the midst of protest, they forgot the violence. There, in that clearing, the crystal note of a song sparrow lifted hesitantly in the hush. And finally, after painful fluttering, another took the song, and then another, the song passing from one bird to another, doubtfully at first, as though some evil thing were being slowly forgotten. Till suddenly they took heart and sang from many throats joyously together as birds are known to sing. They sang because life is sweet and sunlight beautiful. They sang under the brooding shadow of the raven. In simple truth they had forgotten the raven, for they were the singers of life, and not of death.

We are the singers of life, and the first sound many of us heard in life was the cooing of our mother. One of my earliest memories is lying in my mother's arms, looking up at her face, and hearing her sing the lullaby "Mighty like a Rose" to me. The words are ordinary, though the melody is lovely, and the voice and face I remember, beautiful beyond all beauty. It was a lullaby that sang into my heart the love of my mother, ambassador from the heart of the universe.

My parents taught me and my siblings to sing a family grace, which we have taught to our children and they to theirs. That simple song carries something of the family soul down the generations. My daughter Nancy and her husband, Juan Carlos, were in the front seat of their car one day, my then two-and-a-half-year-old grandson Kyle belted in the backseat, holding his milk bottle. They started singing the spiritual "Kum-ba-yah": "Someone's singing, Lord, Kum-ba-yah, / Someone's praying, Lord, Kum-ba-yah," when all at once a little voice came from the backseat, "Someone's drinking milk, Lord, Kum-ba-yah." The kid got it! He understood that the Lord was with him there in the backseat drinking his milk.

We are singers of life. For some of us, "We Shall Overcome" still stirs the soul; others declare "There Is a Balm in Gilead," and many sing of "Amazing Grace." What are your special hymns, chants, movement songs, spirituals? What melodies and what words do you want others to hear and sing at your memorial service? Cynthia Hirni writes: "Songs *without* words proffer reflection. The Native American flute or Japanese folk melodies often accompany my quiet time. A Schubert impromptu, No. 2 in A-flat for piano, heard first in the vaulted space of New York's Riverside Church, is played by recording again and again when words pale and the spirit hungers. I will want it once again at the end. Whale song from the deep of the sea and wolf cry from the forest blend seamlessly with the Paul Winter Consort in concert. . . . Who cannot attend to the sweetness of trumpet and slide trombone when the Canadian Brass rolls its way into 'A Closer Walk with Thee'? Who can sit still when Pete Fountain's clarinet sidles up to the 'Basin Street Blues'? And even without words, Cwm Rhondda prays us forth."

The psalmist cries out for us, "My heart is ready, O God, my heart is ready! I will sing, I will sing praises!"

In *The Brothers Karamazov*, Dostoyevsky portrays Ivan as the cool skeptic, Alyosha the holy one, and Dmitri the passionate lover—each a portion of his own large soul. It is Dmitri who sings the most glorious, outrageous prayer: "For when I do leap into the pit, I go headlong with my heels up, and am pleased to be falling in that degrading attitude, and pride myself upon it. And in the very depths of that degradation I begin a hymn of praise. Let me be accursed. Let me be vile and base, only let me kiss the hem of the veil in which my God is shrouded. Though I may be following the devil, I am Thy son, O Lord, and I love Thee, and I feel the joy without which the world cannot stand."

We are the singers of life, and in the living of these years, from the depths and from the heights, our soul wants to sing its own alleluia in the chorus of creation, "Joyful, Joyful, We Adore Thee."

. . . so we'll live,
And pray, and sing, and tell old tales . . .

In primitive cultures the task of elders was to tell the foundational stories of the tribe: how it came to be, where it came from, where it was going. Tales of primal identity and vocation. The old tales of our nation, religion, or family trace its roots and origins, remind us of who we are, ground us in a communal belonging that gives meaning and dignity and even sacred validation to our own stories. Passing on the wisdom of the tribe is a vital task of creative aging, especially so today, when the socially dominant tales are often told by Hollywood, TV, or politicians replicating whatever is the conventional ideology of the day, or the official, often sanitized cultural story of the region, nation, or society. Telling old tales, sacred stories of our tradition, can provide a desperately needed prophetic or subversive imagination to the cultural scene, inviting us to rediscover ancient stories with power to reveal truth and falsehood, good and evil, power to disrupt and transform us and the world.

One such old tale that has captivated and energized me in these years is the story of two Hebrew midwives as told in the first chapter of Exodus. We may remember the heroines of Exodus 2 (Pharaoh's daughter and Moses' mother and sister), when by canny smuggling, the baby Moses became a basket case and the rebellion was on. But few remember the heroines of Exodus 1. The Egyptian king, fearing a slave rebellion, ordered the Hebrew midwives Puah and Shiprah to kill all male babies at birth. "But the midwives feared God and did not do as the King of Egypt commanded them, but let the male children live" (Ex. 1:17). When confronted by the king, they explained that the Hebrew women were so vigorous in birthing that they and the babies were gone by the time the midwives could get there! What we have here is civil disobedience/divine obedience by women who appeared to be powerless. Their yes to God's command required no to the king's command. They embody and engender in us today a spirituality of resistance to injustice. Their story of subversive imagination encourages our own attempts to confront and subvert unjust institutions or policies in the interest of a deeper vision of human vocation.

The Disobedient Daughter archetype appears frequently in biblical literature and in our common heritage. We have seen how Cordelia's no to her father and king disinherited her but opened a way for Lear's conversion in prison to his own full humanity, where he became for the first time every inch a king, and where he and Cordelia were reconciled.

Emily Dickinson, the only child in her school class who refused to stand up and acknowledge Christ as her savior (because she wasn't sure), stopped going to church at the age of thirty in a time and town where everybody went to church. Accepting her place as a resister and outsider, she went inside, deep into the dark of her own room and soul, where she mined poetic treasure for you and me.

Rosa Parks refused to sit in the back of the bus in

Montgomery one day in 1955, an act that precipitated a boycott that was the beginning of the end of legal segregation in this country. Said an old African-American woman, when one hundred and eighty-one days of walking across town to work instead of taking the bus had won the victory in Montgomery, "My feet are tired, but my soul is rested."

Theresa Kane, Sister of Mercy, stood up in a Philadelphia Cathedral in 1979 to confront the pope on the Roman Catholic Church's lack of justice, much less mercy, to women, seeding the movement for the rights of women in that church. That seed keeps growing in the dark of Vatican disregard, and one day tender green shoots of women's inevitable equality will break through ground that seems as eternally adamant as apartheid once did in South Africa.

Aun Sang Sun Kwi, under house arrest for six years in her homeland, Myanmar (Burma), for courageous leadership of the democracy movement resisting SLORC, the military junta, received the Nobel Peace Prize in 1993, was released in 1995, and is the key figure in the gathering momentum for democracy in that country.

I salute these disobedient daughters and their myriad sisters, known and unknown, some thousands having gathered in Beijing in 1995 to call for the end of economic, political, religious, emotional, physical, and sexual violence against women in every country of the world. There is a "disobedient daughter" slumbering in the soul of every man and woman. If there is a "yes-man" in each of us, there is also a "no-woman." Pentecost (Acts 2) proclaims the amazing grace of the Spirit falling even upon "maidservants," the bottom layer of society. We might remember those "powerless" women who saved the life of Moses, and those other discounted women (Luke 24:10, 11) who first attended the risen Christ, the women of Exodus and Easter.

One seed of all this subversive imagination was sown by two lowly Hebrew midwives—just one old tale out of the thousands of tales in our religious and secular heritage waiting to be mined for their treasures of prophetic discernment and energy. Poetry and fairy tales provided soul energy for a large part of the men's movement of the 1980s and 1990s, bringing thousands of chiefly white middle-class men together in workshops to tell and hear the stories of their lives. The Million Man March on Washington in 1995 brought hundreds of thousands of African-American men together around the text of their burdened history in this country, to find strength and hope for the work of healing their communities today. Small groups gather around texts in schools, churches, synagogues, communities, and homes, seeking inspiration and courage to heal themselves and their corner of creation.

Telling old tales is our métier and our calling in these years of our lives. Some stories will die with us if we do not tell them. Imagine the dark energy hidden in our favorite secular and religious texts, packed with treasure we could mine. Imagine the energy locked into our *lives*, wanting out in the form of stories or letters or family essays, or waiting for some special family or community occasion. We might be self-appointed family historians or tellers of the tales of a congregation or school or neighborhood or whatever human venture has touched us with power and left us with a story to pass on. At our age truth is tasty. No sanitized versions, please. You and I are old enough no longer to be embarrassed by our lives or those of our elders. It is just possible that the telling of old tales that only we can tell might be the most delightful, valuable, and prophetic legacy we can leave those who come after us.

. . . so we'll live,
And pray, and sing, and tell old tales and laugh
At gilded butterflies . . .

There is a deep and seasoned laughter that rolls out at our age, erupting from the belly, uncensored and wild. There's just so much to laugh at, especially oneself. There's a marvelous self-mockery that comes with age, and, occasionally, an emancipation from self-importance.

A couple of years ago I had an appointment with one of our Kirkridge attorneys, a man about twenty-five years my junior. I got to his office at the appointed hour. Time passed, no word from the attorney. I asked the receptionist to inquire about the delay, impatience rising within me. Finally, after waiting forty minutes past the hour, I was informed by a secretary that the attorney was involved in an appointment he could not terminate soon, and that we needed to set up another appointment. I got angry, leaned towards the secretary, and told her to tell the attorney I didn't appreciate having wasted over an hour of my time, and I wished he had had the courtesy to come out and tell me himself. I left in a huff. Another appointment was made, and the attorney apologized for having stood me up. But it was days later before I realized I had been filled with self-importance on that day. Who was this *young* lawyer, not to be able and willing to see *me*? So childish and silly on my part. It astonishes me how often I get an attack of self-importance and expect others to treat me like a VIP. Deeper than matters of courtesy in such situations is gaining perspective on our own human dignity, which is neither enhanced by the attentions of others nor diminished by their absence. At our age we can laugh a little at ourselves and others playing out the human comedy.

There is a (perhaps apocryphal) story about President George Bush's ceremonial visit to a nursing home shortly after Clinton was elected. The manager of the institution, a woman, took him around to greet people. Peering at an elderly man, Bush said, "Do you know who I am?" The elderly man pointed at the manager and said, "No, but she does." Touché! At our age it is more important for *us* to know who we are than for others to know who we are.

At the same time, as attorney Charles Rembar reminded us earlier (in Chapter 4), there is also a special pleasure deriving from the canniness that comes with age, the hard-won ability to take unfair advantage of those who are younger, less wily, and with less street smarts. Old has earned a certain right to be outrageous and outraged. A review of eighty-four-year-old Herbert Block's book *Herblock: A Cartoonist's Life* is highlighted by the words: "Herblock at 84 is still outraged, still at the top of his form." Still outraged, "still crazy after all these years." The gift of satire increases with age, as does the gift of emancipation from conventional mores. At our age, freed of obsolete inhibitions, we often can say and do what we want. What are they going to do to us? Career advancement, social climbing, proving oneself, pleasing people, are losing their luster. And good riddance.

And there's the pleasure that accompanies those occasions when our special knowledge is recognized and sought. Broadway playwright and screenwriter Garson Kanin spoke to correspondent Morley Safer on the television program *60 Minutes* about ageism. He said, "There's a story of a town in Connecticut that lost its power, had a complete outage. And they simply could not repair it [until] someone remembered that there was an old, old electrical engineer who had installed the system in the first place, and he was living in some retirement community, and they sent for him. And he came along and he got a little mallet out and he went tap, tap on a switch and all the lights came on. He sent the town a bill for $1000.02 . . . itemized as follows: Tapping, 2 cents. Knowing where to tap, $1000." Right on! Oh, the pleasures and rewards of tapping into our own wisdom and, now and then, having the last laugh.

When Lear invites us to laugh at gilded butterflies, he may be expressing the folly of trying to gild a creature as ineffably beautiful as a butterfly. Not a lily, not a butterfly. Gentle laughter at our penchant for human presumption. Or as Jungian psychotherapist and educator Helen Luke puts it, "It is the laughter of pure delight in beauty—beauty of which the golden butterfly is the perfect symbol—a fleeting, ephemeral thing, passing on the wind, eternally reborn from the earthbound worm, the fragile yet omnipotent beauty of the present moment." Or it might be the laughter erupting from what you do for the sheer joy of it: reading, watching birds and butterflies, going to a museum, listening to music, playing golf, dancing, gathering flowers, skiing, making love, playing with your computer, gardening, flying in a glider, considering the lilies, studying the wisdom of the flowers. All the ways we take time for paradise now.

The other day I laughed out loud upon reading an article in *Nature Conservancy* magazine about the resplendent quetzal, a small bird whose radiant green and red plumage and elegant three-foot-long tail feathers have entranced pre-Columbian cultures and twentieth-century birdwatchers. You should see the pictures of this outrageously designed and colored bird! The incredible imagination of natural selection or whomever. I keep it to myself that I am so taken with this bird, not wanting to appear dotty, until I remember that it doesn't matter anymore. In some cases, like this, dotty is beautiful!

There comes to a few of those who face death, whether in old age or earlier, whether due to illness or danger, a certain insouciance, a lightness of being arising from the awareness of one's mortality. In the winter of 1968 Martin Luther King Jr. was on a flight to Atlanta. One of the reporters on the plane asked him about his experiences in jail, and when he had feared for his life. King said he was frightened the night he and his colleague Ralph Abernathy were speaking in Philadelphia, Mississippi, where the three young civil-rights workers James Chaney, Andrew Goodman, and Michael Schwerner had been murdered in the summer of 1964. Sheriff Lawrence Rainey, one of the principal suspects in the triple killings, stood right behind him on the platform.

"King laughed as he recalled the moment when he had said that the people were behind them in their fight and Rainey had growled in his ear: 'That's right, I'm behind you!' King shook his head at the thought. 'Well, it came time to pray and I sure did not want to close my eyes! Ralph said he prayed with his eyes open!' Everyone in the plane laughed and then slowly stopped and became quiet. The film men put away their camera and sound equipment; they were cinema verité men and they knew they could not hope to catch a better sequence that day, just as I felt that I had the key to Dr. King's style: praying with his eyes open is what he does all the time."

This article by Jose Yglesias was published in the *New York Times Magazine* on Sunday, March 31, 1968. Five days later King was shot and killed in Memphis at the age of thirty-nine.

One remembers Yeats's words:

No longer in Lethean foliage caught,
Begin the preparation for your death
And from the fortieth winter by that thought
Test every work of intellect or faith
And everything that your own hands have wrought,
And call those works extravagance of breath
That are not suited for such men as come
Proud, open-eyed and laughing to the tomb.

. . . and hear poor rogues
Talk of court news; and we'll talk with them too.
Who loses and who wins; who's in, who's out;

Shakespeare gives us an image of listening to "poor rogues," those still caught up in the intrigues, the wheeling and dealing politics of the court. Lear used to be such a poor rogue himself, though in a position to command and tell, not needing or caring to listen, much less to hear. But now, freed from his ego agenda through all his suffering, he listens with empathy, talking "with them too," not separated from the concerns of their court world, but no longer caught in its net of power seeking, his listening untainted by contempt or boredom.

My friend Peter's "court" scene is Wall Street. He's a stock analyst. We were talking once about addictions, trying to get a handle on our own. He said, "I'm addicted to news: the latest newspaper or TV account of what's happening on Wall Street. I'm greedy for news, want it all day long and until I fall in bed at night." Yet Peter reads novels, history, poetry, and other literature and takes a sardonic view of things. It is as though he watches himself from a slight distance—at the Wall Street trough feeding frenzy of stock news—and gives himself an inner nod to take it all with a grain of salt, even as, consciously, he internalizes the ticker-tape news for optimum strategy in selling and buying.

For twenty years my "court" scene was Kirkridge, where I fed, in my daily tempest-in-a-teapot context, on engrossing news of staff, retreatants, leaders, board members, colleagues, major contributors, the wider constituency. Which leaders are "hot," which are not? What events register high numbers, which low? What's happening in board and staff politics? Now my "court" scene is the gossip of a local congregation, community, and neighborhood. And, of course, the wider family has been and is a scene of captivation, and the daily *New York Times* with all the news that's fit to print of the fate of people and nations. I'm not yet with Lear in practicing nonattachment. I'm still caught up in right and wrong, good and evil, heroes and villains on the political scene. I am a hopeless partisan and advocate, and therefore, not a very good mediator. I still care who wins and who loses, and rage according to who gets in, who's thrown out. I love the comment of the dying, corrupt curmudgeon of the novel *The Last Hurrah*: that the political fortunes of an enemy had declined because his intention to deceive was not matched by his capacity to do so.

Yet a secret smile lurks, and somehow it hurts a little less now if my side doesn't win, and the surge of victory fades sooner than it used to. There grows in me some recognition that all this is a matter of penultimate concern, that pendulums swing, that "all is vanity." And occasionally I find myself in a state of bemusement. Regrettably, the last thing to go is self-righteousness. The politically passionate almost always carry a big load of arrogance and even contempt. So disclaimers are salutary. I find it useful now and then to reread this poem found by Helen Gilbert, now eighty-eight years old, when she was going through her mother's things after her death.

> I dreamed death came the other night
> And heaven's gate swung wide.
> With kindly grace, an Angel ushered me inside.
> And there, to my astonishment,
> Stood folks I'd known on earth—
> Some I'd judged and labeled as
>   "Unfit" or "Little Worth."

Indignant words rose to my lips
   but never were set free
For every face showed stunned surprise . . .
No one expected ME!

I notice that I am listening to my children tell the pains and joys of their lives with a willingness mainly to listen, seldom to advise. I know now that I do not know what is best for them, that they have to make their own decisions and then live with them. So I am more relaxed, no longer feeling responsible for their health or success or happiness. They know I love them, so they can run whatever they choose of their lives by me with confidence that I am, usually, a sympathetic listener. We can still communicate displeasure with silence or long pauses, or with "Really?" But our main job is to listen. And what a lovely relief no longer to have to try to figure out how they should run their lives.

I have never regarded myself, nor have others regarded me, as a good listener, because I have usually been doing my number on people, pursuing my agenda of the moment. But now, as I understand that listening is part of my vocation in age, there seem to come frequent opportunities to do so, and though I am a rookie listener, I may be improving enough to last the season. In these years we are moving into the ranks of those who, often unpaid, are trusted listeners in our various court scenes. If we were not accustomed to suffer fools gladly, we may begin to recognize our own foolishness and think more kindly of those who suffered us over the years, gladly or sadly. We begin to understand that we too have been clowning around in this multiringed human circus, and that a good clown gets us to laugh at ourselves, as a good listener helps us to hear ourselves. So we're willing to "talk with them too."

And take upon's the mystery of things,
As if we were God's spies.

One hesitates to probe or exegete this glorious summation. These words capture the essence of what it means to be human, to embrace, beyond all that we can comprehend, the abiding mystery at the heart of the universe. To take upon the mystery of things is to wear it like a shawl or cloak, to put on a cloud of unknowing, to live into a luminous darkness. We may experience the mystery as random and contingent, implacable, as silent as stone in the face of human sorrow. We may question our way into a whirlwind of no answers, like Job, or feel forsaken, like Jesus. But there may also come moments when the veil is thin and we know we are known. The mystery is never revealed, always elusive, pregnant with surprise: as the Holy Spirit, in the words of poet Gerard Manley Hopkins, "over the bent / World broods with warm breast and with ah! bright wings." Poets, lunatics, and lovers tell about the mystery in their languages of strange and awe-ful wonder. The closest some of us can get to it may be the secrets lovers share with each other: when a familiar landscape is noticed or a tryst remembered, when we breathe in the fragrance of honeysuckle on a certain country road, when we know that whatever happens we will be there for each other, that where the beloved is, there is home, and that beyond the beloved, the great Lover abides.

The mystery emanates grace upon grace. Author Frederick Buechner writes, "A crazy, holy grace I have called it. Crazy because whoever could have predicted it? Who can ever foresee the crazy now and when and where of a grace that wells up out of the lostness and pain of the world and of our own inner worlds? And holy because these moments of grace come ultimately from farther away than Oz and deeper down than doom, holy because they heal and hallow."

Taking on the mystery is yielding to grace, letting go of all explanations, analyses, ideologies, self-images, images of God, agendas, expectations. Taking on the mystery is undergoing the finitude of years, hallowing diminishments, and living into the solitude of our own integrity. Taking on the mystery is undergoing the pain of learning that there are no empires favored by the Holy One: not the Roman, or the British, or the Soviet, or the American. Taking on the mystery is undergoing the grief of understanding that there are no theologies favored by the Holy One: not communism or capitalism, not Islam, Judaism, or Christianity. Taking on the mystery is acknowledging that we cannot name the mystery, though we try, we cannot claim the mystery, though we do. The mystery names and claims us, inviting us to take it upon ourselves as if we were God's spies.

One who sought to spy out the mystery was Norman Maclean, retired professor of English literature at the University of Chicago. In his youth a woodsman and firefighter, at age seventy-four he undertook to understand all he could of the mystery of a 1949 forest fire in which a crew of fifteen Smokejumpers, the U.S. Forest Service's elite airborne fire-fighters, stepped into the sky above a remote forest fire in the Montana wilderness. Less than two hours after their jump, all but three of these men were dead or fatally burned. Why? What happened? What went wrong? Maclean spent the last fourteen years of his life researching the story of these young firefighters who "hadn't learned to count the odds and to sense they might owe the universe a tragedy." He invited two survivors to return to the scene of the disaster and, at risk to his own safety, accompanied them to the ridge where they had escaped into life while their friends burned in death. It became Maclean's magnificent obsession to wrest meaning out of the mystery of this disaster, a vocation inculcated by his father, a Presbyterian minister, who said in his hearing, "One of the chief privileges of man is to speak up for the universe." Maclean was also moved by the intuition that giving his last years to researching and telling the tragic story of the young firefighters was at the same time the vehicle for understanding and gathering the final meanings of his own life story, including his wife's death from cancer. Maclean's last words in the book are these: "I, an old man, have written this fire report. Among other things, it was important to me, as an exercise for my old age, to enlarge my knowledge and spirit so I could accompany young men whose lives I might have lived on their way to death. I have climbed where they climbed, and in my time I have fought fire and inquired into its nature. In addition, I have tried to get a better understanding of myself and those close to me, many of them now dead. Perhaps it is not odd, at the end of this tragedy where nothing much was left of the elite who came from the sky but courage struggling for oxygen, that I have often found myself thinking of my wife on her brave and lonely way to death."

Maclean was a faithful spy of the God in whom he believed and in whose mystery he rests. Lear invites us also to be co-conspirators with God. What an assignment! Spies are subversive, keeping and finding out secrets, as in children's games: Who's it? How do you get to the Secret Garden? Where's the buried treasure? Reconciled with his beloved Cordelia, Lear is now winging his way out of his valley of sorrows, forgetting for the moment the tragedy happening around him. He is becoming like a child again, playful, hopeful, a singer of life in the face of death. He welcomes us into the exotic, erotic world of spies in the service of the bittersweet mystery.

The apostle Paul wrote that faith, hope, and love abide in the abyss of mystery, and that the greatest of these is love. If we were to live as if this were so, how might we slip love into a situation or find out how a person or institution might be vulnerable to love? We can be wired with love, for love, tapping into the electricity of the Spirit, living as if Love were the name of the mystery of things. It is a gamble, just as living as if Nothing were the name of the mystery is a gamble. We might begin to notice ordinary, daily things with the curiosity of a child, looking through the wise eyes of our heart, getting into the spirit of the game, and going down the street on alert for a miracle.

E. B. White watched his wife Katharine planning the planting of bulbs in her garden in the last autumn of her life and later wrote about it: "There was something comical yet touching in her bedraggled appearance. . . . The small hunched-over figure, her studied absorption in the implausible notion that there would be yet another spring, oblivious to the ending of her own days, which she knew perfectly well was near at hand, sitting there with her detailed chart under those dark skies in dying October, calmly plotting the resurrection."

There is room for all of us in the resurrection conspiracy, the company of those who plant seeds of hope in dark times of grief or oppression, going about the living of these years until, no one knows quite how, the tender Easter shoots appear.

Questions for pondering:

What's on your "menu"?

When do you pray?

What stories of your own life or your family or community are dying to be told?

How do you experience the mystery?

SOURCES

Biblical quotations in this book on pages 30, 42, 56, 75, 148, 166, 176, 178 are taken from the Revised Standard Version, published in 1946–52 by Thomas Nelson and Sons, New York. Biblical quotations on pages 55, 58, 104 and 167 are taken from the New Revised Standard Version Bible, published in 1989 by Zondervan Bible Publishers, Grand Rapids, Michigan.

Introduction

p. 2. Betty Friedan, *The Fountain of Age* (New York: Simon and Schuster, 1993), 19; Daniel Levinson, *The Seasons of a Man's Life* (New York: Alfred A. Knopf, 1978), 34–37; Jane R. Prétat, *Coming to Age* (Toronto: Inner City, 1994), 7–11; Gail Sheehy, *New Passages* (New York: Random House, 1995), 343.

Chapter I: Waking Up

p. 7. The Bustle in a House: Emily Dickinson, in *The Complete Poems of Emily Dickinson*, ed. Thomas H. Johnson (Boston: Little, Brown, 1960), 489.
p. 10. There is the fear: Marie-Louise von Franz, *Projection and Re-collection in Jungian Psychology* (London: Open Court, 1980), 30–31.

Jonathan Schell, *The Fate of the Earth* (New York: Alfred A. Knopf, 1982), 144.

p. 12. Georges Simenon, *When I Was Old* (New York: Harcourt Brace Jovanovich, 1970).

p. 13. John Updike, *Rabbit at Rest* (New York: Alfred A. Knopf, 1990).

p. 14. When my friends threw: Friedan, *Fountain of Age*, 13.

p. 19. For sixty years: Rumi, "The Music," in John Moyne and Coleman Barks, eds., *Open Secret* (Putney, Vt.: Threshold, 1984), 74.

pp. 27–28. The dancing old women: Clarissa Pinkola Estes, "The Dancing Grandmas," *Common Boundary*, March–April 1993, pp. 38–41.

Chapter 2: Embracing Sorrow

p. 29. What is sorrow for?: Robert Bly, "Ramage for Awakening Sorrow," in Stephen Brigidi, ed., *Angels in Pompeii* (New York: Ballantine, 1992).

p. 32. common memory: Lawrence L. Langer, *Holocaust Testimonies: The Ruins of Memory*, as reviewed in Davis S. Wyman, *New York Times Book Review*, April 21, 1991, p. 7.

p. 33. My heart is moved: Adrienne Rich, "Natural Resources," in *The Dream of a Common Language* (New York: W. W. Norton, 1978), 67.

pp. 37–38. Sometimes I have: Anne Tyler, *Saint Maybe* (New York: Alfred A. Knopf, 1991), 181.

pp. 40–41. I became the client: Tom Stoddard, quoted in David Margolick, "At the Bar," *New York Times*, Law, February 5, 1993.

pp. 41–42. listen to garble: David Dodson Gray, *I Want to Remember: A Son's Reflection on His Mother's Alzheimer Journey* (Wellesley, Mass.: Roundtable), 54, 64, 115, 125.

p. 43. Drop, drop—in our sleep: Aeschylus, *Agamemnon*, tr. Edith Hamilton, in John Massner, ed., *A Treasury of the Theatre* (New York: Simon and Schuster, 1935), 13.

pp. 44–45. came a contralto voice: William Styron, *Darkness Visible* (New York: Random House, 1990), 66, 67, 79–80.

pp. 45–46. You leant heavily into: Nancy Raines, text of master's thesis dance performance at Smith College, piece titled *Haloweyo*.

p. 47. Deep in a time: Howard Nemerov, "Lines and Circularities: On Hearing Casals' Recording of the Sixth Suite," in *The Collected Poems of Howard Nemerov* (Chicago: University of Chicago Press, 1977), 416.

Chapter 3: Savoring Blessedness

p. 49. My fiftieth year had: William Butler Yeats, *Selected Poems and Three Plays*, ed. M. L. Rosenthal (New York: Macmillan, 1986), 141–42.

pp. 51–53. Natan Sharansky, *Fear No Evil* (New York: Random House, 1988).

p. 53. Your solitudes utter: Denise Levertov, "Poet and Person," in *Candles in Babylon* (New York: New Directions, 1978), 6.

p. 56. Philip Roth, *Patrimony* (New York: Simon and Schuster, 1991).

p. 58. And you, my father: Dylan Thomas, "Do Not Go Gentle into That Good Night," in *The Poems of*

Dylan Thomas, ed. Daniel Jones (New York: New Directions, 1971), 207–208.

pp. 61–63. It happened during: Robert Raines, *To Kiss the Joy*, Nashville, Tenn.: Abingdon, 1983), 78.

pp. 63–65. I looked through: Lewis Hyde, *The Gift* (New York: Random House, 1979), 281.

p. 69. I met Jeannie Roth: Friedan, *Fountain of Age*, 584.

p. 71. To see the world: William Blake, "Auguries of Innocence," in *William Blake: Selected Poems and Letters*, ed. J. Bronowski (New York: Penguin, 1958), 67.

p. 72. When I was brought down: Oscar Wilde quotation from Robert Raines, *Creative Brooding* (New York: Macmillan, 1977), 86.

pp. 73–74. I am experiencing: *New York Times*, International Edition, December 26, 1989, p. A19.

Chapter 4: Re-imagining Work

p. 77. Whatever is foreseen: Wendell Berry, *Sabbaths*, [tenth poem], (San Francisco: North Point, 1987), 19

p. 82. hot from the fire: Levinson, *Seasons*, 228.

But we are also: Thomas Moore, *Care of the Soul* (New York: HarperCollins, 1992), 182.

p. 84. Robert Raines, *Going Home* (New York: Harper and Row, 1979).

It is in the nature: Moore, *Care of the Soul*, 44.

p. 86. a sculpted creativity: Levinson, *Seasons*, 228.

He writes in his book: (New York: Hyperion, 1995), 4.

p. 88. The thing to do: Charles Rembar, "The Joy of Old," *New York Times Magazine*, Oct. 27, 1991, pp. 24ff.

p. 89. As the game unfolds: Jackson, *Sacred Hoops*, 203.

pp. 89–90. reputation as star maker: Barbara Jepson, "She Helps Fiddlers Help Themselves," *New York Times*, July 26, 1992, p. H19.

pp. 90–91. takes on whatever trouble: Colman McCarthy, "From the Eye of the Storm," Washington Post Writers Group, July–August 1992, p. 63.

p. 92. emancipated innocence: Allan B. Chinen, *In the Ever After*, (Wilmette, Ill.: Chiron, 1989), 78.

I never have an: Martin E. Marty, "While You Were Out . . . ," *The Christian Century*, May 20–27, 1992, p. 567.

p. 93. William Blake, "The Marriage of Heaven and Hell," in *Blake: Poems*, ed. J. Bronowski, 94.

pp. 96–97. The ultimate work: Moore, *Care of the Soul*, 199.

p. 98. I am called in: Bill Wylie Kellermann, *A Keeper of The Word* (Grand Rapids, Mich.: William B. Eerdmans, 1994), 5.

So, friends, every day: Wendell Berry, "Manifesto: The Mad Farmer Liberation Front," in *The Country of Marriage* (New York: Harcourt Brace Jovanovich, 1971), 16.

p. 99. The new cosmology teaches: Matthew Fox, *The Re-invention of Work* (San Francisco: Harper-Collins, 1994), 61.

pp. 101–102. transcend notions of accountability: A. Bartlett Giamatti, *Take Time for Paradise* (New York: Summit, 1989), 19ff.

Chapter 5: Nurturing Intimacy

p. 103. But that other: Denise Levertov, "Lovers (II):

Reminder," in *Oblique Prayers* (New York: New Directions, 1981), 13.

p. 107. rage: Friedan, *Fountain of Age*, 261.

p. 109. I was offered many: Mary Catherine Bateson, *With a Daughter's Eye* (New York: William Morrow, 1984), 72–73, 81.

pp. 110–12. as the love that: Rainer Maria Rilke, *Letters to a Young Poet*, trans. M. D. Herter Norton (New York: W. W. Norton, 1934), 59.

p. 112. a man and a woman: Robert Bly, "A Third Body," in *Loving a Woman in Two Worlds* (Garden City, N.Y.: Doubleday, 1985), 19.

pp. 112–13. He who binds to: William Blake, "Eternity," as quoted in John Bartlett, ed., *Familiar Quotations* (Boston: Little, Brown 1955), 386.

p. 114. "diminished erotic response": Aaron Kipnis, *Knights Without Armor* (Los Angeles: Jeremy P. Tarcher, 1991), 45.

p. 115. I told her, whatever: Friedan, *Fountain of Age*, 271–72.

pp. 116–17. Here on my window: Loren Eiseley, "The Cardinals," in *Notes of an Alchemist* (New York: Charles Scribner's Sons, 1974), 93.

p. 117. The family the soul: Thomas Moore, *Soul Mates* (San Francisco: HarperCollins, 1994), 71–72.

p. 122. Friendship doesn't ask for: Moore, *Soul Mates*, 95.

pp. 125–26. How is it that: Morton Hunt, "The Age of Intimacy" *New York Times Magazine*, About Men, April 10, 1994, pp. 28, 30.

pp. 126–27. We must continually beware: Friedan, *Fountain of Age*, 290.

pp. 127–28. A few months before: James B. Nelson, *Body Theology* (Louisville, Ky.: Westminster/John Knox, 1992), 103–104.

p. 130. take this beauty into: Maria Jose Hobday, "Strung Memories," in *Parabola: Myth and the Quest for Meaning*, IV:4 (1979), p. 4.

pp. 130–32. decided that, because slave: Toni Morrison, *Beloved* (New York: Alfred A. Knopf, 1987), 87–88.

Chapter 6: Seeking Forgiveness

p. 133. For thee, oppressed king: William Shakespeare, *King Lear*, in *The Complete Plays and Poems of William Shakespeare*, eds. William Allan Neilson and Charles Harvis Hill (Cambridge, Mass.: Houghton Mifflin, 1942), 1175.

p. 136. The blessing that the: Helen Luke, *Old Age* (New York: Parabola Books, 1987), 27.

p. 139. We had fought throughout: Sam Osherson, *Finding Our Fathers* (New York: Free Press, 1986), 194–95.

p. 141. Many sibling relationships do: Francine Klagsbrun, *Mixed Feelings* (New York: Bantam, 1992), 284–86.

pp. 144–45. was already following the: William Kennedy, *Ironweed* (New York: Viking, 1983), 16–19.

p. 146. A glimpse of his: Max Frankel, "McNamara's Retreat," in *New York Times Book Review*, April 16, 1995, pp. 1, 24.

p. 146. A great and almost: Robert McAfee Brown, letter to editor of *New York Times*, April 13, 1995, p. 24.

p. 148. Those of us who: Walter Brueggemann, "Candor and Coherence in Faith: A Study of Psalms," lecture at Kirkridge Retreat Center, Bangor, Pa., January 14, 1985.

p. 151. Owabi, an unambigious word: Sheryl WuDunn, *New York Times*, News of the Week in Review, August 20, 1995, p. 2.

p. 152. I learned in Nicaragua: The Amanecida Collective, *Revolutionary Forgiveness* (Maryknoll, N.Y.: Orbis, 1987), 80.

p. 153. I can tell you: Francis X. Clines, "A Joyous Day of Lining Up to Vote for Mandela," *New York Times*, Late New York Edition, April 28, 1994.

Like a coronation: "Mandela Ends Triumphant Visit to Britain," *New York Times*, International Edition, July 13, 1996, p. 5.

pp. 155–56. The pavements swarmed with: Yevgeny Yevtushenko, *A Precocious Autobiography*, trans. Andrew R. MacAndrew (New York: E. P. Dutton, 1963), 22–25. Used by permission of Dutton Signet, a division of Penguin Books USA, Inc.

p. 157. Nothing worth doing is: Reinhold Niebuhr, *The Irony of American History* (New York: Charles Scribner's Sons, 1952), 63.

Chapter 7: Taking On the Mystery

p. 159. So we'll live: Shakespeare, *King Lear*, 1175.

pp. 159–61. Exercise designed by Rabbi Zalman Schachter-Shalomi author, with Ronald S. Miller, of *From Aging to Saging* (New York: Warner, 1995).

pp. 164–65. Early in the morning: Alexander Solzhenitsyn, *Cancer Ward*, trans. Nicholas Bethell and

David Burg (New York: Farrar, Straus and Giroux, 1969), 484–90.

p. 166. The description of the: John Biersdorf, *Healing of Purpose* (Nashville, Tenn.: Abingdon, 1985), 99.

To pray is: Abraham Heschel, *Man's Quest for God* (New York: Charles Scribner's Sons, 1954), 13.

p. 167. Hope is an orientation: Vaclav Havel, *Disturbing the Peace* (New York: Alfred A. Knopf, 1990), 181–86.

p. 167–68. History belongs to the: Walter Wink, *Engaging the Powers* (Minneapolis: Fortress, 1992), 299.

pp. 168–69. Nothing is as secret: Herrymon Maurer, *Simple Prayer* (publication data unavailable).

pp. 170–71. We should sink eternally: Matthew Fox, *Breakthrough: Meister Eckhart's Creation Spirituality in New Translation* (Garden City, N.Y.: Doubleday, 1980), 179–80.

p. 171 David McCullough, *Truman* (New York: Simon and Schuster, 1992), 986.

I stood in front: Marlise Simons, "In a French Cave: Wildlife Scenes from a Long-Gone World," *New York Times*, January 24, 1995, p. C10.

p. 173. You see, I told: Roberta Smith, *New York Times*, December 23, 1993, pp. C7, C12.

Lone, inactive males start: Diane Ackerman, *A Natural History of the Senses* (New York: Random House, 1991), 200.

pp. 173–74. When I awoke: Loren Eiseley, "The Judgment of the Birds," in *The Immense Journey*, (New York: Random House, 1956), 174–75.

p. 176. Songs *without* words proffer: Cynthia Hirni, "How Sweet the Sound," *Ridgeleaf* #184 (May 1991) (Bangor, Pa.: Kirkridge Retreat Center), 19.

For when I do: Fyodor Dostoyevsky, *The Brothers Karamasov*, trans. Constance Garnett (New York: Random House, 1950), 126.

p. 179. My feet are tired: Howell Raines, *My Soul Is Rested* (New York: G. P. Putnam's Sons, 1977), 61.

p. 182. Herblock at 84: Edward Sorel, "The Pillar of the Post," *New York Times Book Review*, October 17, 1993, p. 13.

p. 183. There's a story: Excerpted from Frank Coffey, *60 Minutes: 25 Years of Television's Finest Hour* (New York: General Publishing Group, 1993). On October 8, 1978, Broadway playwright and screenwriter Garson Kanin spoke to correspondent Morley Safer on ageism. (This appeared in *Modern Maturity*, February–March 1994.)

It is the laughter: Luke, *Old Age*, 29.

p. 184. *Nature Conservancy* magazine, November–December 1993.

p. 185. King laughed as he: Jose Yglesias, "Dr. King's March on Washington, Part II," *New York Times Magazine*, March 31, 1968, p. 70.

p. 185. No longer in Lethean: William Butler Yeats, "Vacillation," in *Poems and Plays*, ed. M. L. Rosenthal, 141.

p. 187. Edwin O'Connor, *The Last Hurrah* (Boston: Little, Brown, 1956), 380.

pp. 187–88. I dreamed death came: Quoted by Morton Kelsey, *Through Defeat to Victory* (New York: Continuum, 1993), 114.

p. 189. Over the bent world: Gerard Manley Hopkins, "God's Grandeur," in *Poems of Gerard Manley Hopkins*, ed. Robert Bridges (London: Oxford University Press, 1918), 26.

p. 190. A crazy, holy grace: Frederick Buechner, *The Sacred Journey* (New York: Harper and Row, 1982), 57.

pp. 190–92. hadn't learned to count: Norman Maclean, *Young Men and Fire* (Chicago: University of Chicago Press, 1992), 19, 216, 300–301.

pp. 192–93. There was something comical: E. B. White, introduction to Katharine S. White, *Onward and Upward in the Garden* (New York: Farrar, Straus and Giroux, 1979), xix.